This book is accessible, funny and hugely helpful. It will ~~~ your vision of a life lived fruitfully for God in everyday circumstances. More importantly, it will deepen your appetite to live such a life, and your faith that in Christ you can.
*Graham Cray, Archbishops' Missioner and Team Leader of Fresh Expressions 2009–2014*

This is a must-read, especially if you are wondering whether your daily life matters to God and can make a difference. Mark's book is not only real, honest and funny, but also extremely helpful. You won't want to put it down.
*Sharon Dirckx, tutor and lecturer at the Oxford Centre for Christian Apologetics and author of* Why?

What sounds loud and clear in the pages of this book is Mark's deep desire to see Christians set free to live fully for the glory of God, wherever they are. Where Monday mornings can be as filled with worshipful focus as Sunday mornings. For too long, mission has been seen as the preserve of a handful of specialists. We know this isn't true, but still, church culture celebrates mainly those who are directly paid to do 'God's work'. Mark's book offers us a beautiful revolution – what if all of us recognized our equality of calling, that God intends for all of us to be his missionaries right where we are: pastry-chef, plumber or party-planner?
*Rachel Gardner, speaker, writer on youth issues and President of the Girl's Brigade*

This is a tremendously warm and practical book, filled with encouraging, achievable examples from every area of life. There really is something for everybody: as I read, I couldn't stop thinking of friends, relatives and others who I would love to recommend it to. More than that, this is a book rooted in prayer and built on a strong Christian foundation.
*Ram Gidoomal, Chairman of the Lausanne Movement and of Traidcraft plc*

There is surely no more urgent issue for today's church than how to motivate and equip *every* Christian to work and witness for God's kingdom. This wise, thoughtful and practical book should challenge and encourage all of us who follow Christ to live more effectively for him in whatever place or position we have been called to. Heartily recommended!
*Revd Canon J.John, author and speaker*

Fed up of feeling like a failure when it comes to living for Jesus? Think missional fruitfulness means you have to tell someone the whole gospel, and nothing less than that 'counts'? Mark Greene's *Fruitfulness on the Frontline* is the reassurance you need. His 6Ms will help you start to celebrate where you are already bearing kingdom fruit, as well as gently encouraging you to look for new opportunities to share the Jesus-life on your frontline. Great for use in churches or for reading on your own!
*Chloe Lynch, leader, LifeGiving Church and visiting lecturer, London School of Theology*

An excellent book. Full of real life and rich wisdom. It's easy to read and will have a lasting impact on our daily lives.
*Mark Melluish, Director of New Wine and Tear Fund*

A fantastic book. Clear, well argued, brilliantly illustrated from both Scripture and modern life, and above all, passionate. Mark, like the great Old Testament prophets, is urging us with both wit and wisdom to get the church out of the buildings and into the world God loves. Both biblical and practical, this should be studied by individuals, home groups and churches. And then acted upon. Truly a word for today.
*Mike Pilavachi, Soul Survivor*

This book took me by surprise! Not because I didn't expect it to be an inspiring read – no, I've always been a huge fan of Mark's books and so I knew that I was going to enjoy vivid storytelling, quirky humour, a healthy seasoning of Scripture and down-to-earth practical application. And I wasn't disappointed. This book is *all* those things and more. But the thing that took me by surprise was this: I felt like it spoke to my very soul. As I turned each page, something in the deepest part of me knew that this is what I'm called to *be* – this is what we're all called to *be*. Fruitful! And it felt possible. Attainable. Essential – for me and for God's world. So, with open hearts, *read* it. With God's help, *be* it. With eyes full of wonder and gratitude, *see* it.

*Matt Summerfield, Chief Executive of Urban Saints and Senior Pastor, Hitchin Christian Centre*

This is as refreshing as a mango smoothie; it is a delight to take in and it is good for you. The warm and friendly tone draws you into its human and humorous reflections on being a follower of Jesus, whatever your day-to-day routine involves. It gives attractive and generous insights into being a Christian and offers wisdom and encouragement to all who might read it. There is something beguilingly accessible about the way it is written, and yet there are profound biblical truths presented with wit and charm. An engaging read, with practical meaning and considerable value to all who would seek understanding on living the Jesus way. This is the book to read if you need fresh inspiration for discipleship and renewed encouragement to be a witness to the love God shows us in Christ.

*Revd Dianne Tidball, author and Regional Minister, East Midland Baptist Association*

Mark Greene is a brilliant communicator. This book will be invaluable in helping people to live in the present, taking the opportunities ordinary life presents, and to live what Mark calls 'a life well lived in Christ'.

*Revd Dr Graham Tomlin, Dean, St Mellitus College*

No-one I know speaks and writes more passionately or persuasively about whole-life frontline discipleship than Mark Greene. The shrewd, biblical framework he develops here – with all his characteristic freshness and humour – makes this a truly transformational read which opened my mind to a rich feast of God-honouring, culture-changing, life-enhancing possibilities in which the ordinary can become important and the mundane magnificent. Here is a superb antidote to mediocrity or discouragement for any Christian, at any age or stage, who means business with God.
*His Honour Judge David Turner QC, Circuit Judge*

This book has filled me with excitement and made me want to jump off my sofa and get on with my life – to be open to all the things that God wants to do through me with the people and places that I'm going to be involved with today. I hope it'll inspire you to do the same!
*Dr Ruth Valerio, Churches and Theology Director, A Rocha UK*

This is a very dangerous book. If you read it, anything might happen. In particular, you might find that you have to let God out of the safe box you've got him in and let him come with you to your 'frontline' – to the places where you spend most of your life. God doesn't live in churches, and neither do we. God has work for every single one of us to do in those places where we actually live and work. The only question is whether we are prepared to be God's employees.
*Jane Williams, theology tutor at St Mellitus College*

# FRUITFULNESS
## ON THE FRONTLINE.

For Gail

wishing you an joy + the inspiration of
the Spirit in all -

with thanks for your
heartening worship.

Mark Greene

# Mark Greene

# FRUITFULNESS ON THE FRONTLINE.

## Making a difference where you are

INTER-VARSITY PRESS
Norton Street, Nottingham NG7 3HR, England
Email: ivp@ivpbooks.com
Website: www.ivpbooks.com

*First published 2014*
*Reprinted 2014*

**British Library Cataloguing in Publication Data**
A catalogue record for this book is available from the British Library.

ISBN: 978–1–78359–125–1
ePub: 978–1–78359–126–8
Mobi: 978–1–78359–127–s5

Set in Dante 12/15pt
Typeset in Great Britain by CRB Associates, Potterhanworth, Lincolnshire
Printed in Great Britain by Ashford Colour Press Ltd, Gosport, Hampshire

*Inter-Varsity Press publishes Christian books that are true to the Bible and that
communicate the gospel, develop discipleship and strengthen the church for its mission
in the world.*

*Inter-Varsity Press is closely linked with the Universities and Colleges Christian
Fellowship, a student movement connecting Christian Unions in universities and colleges
throughout Great Britain, and a member movement of the International Fellowship of
Evangelical Students. Website: www.uccf.org.uk*

I will sing of the LORD's great love for ever;
with my mouth I will make your faithfulness known
through all generations.

Psalm 89:1

You did not choose me,
but I chose you and appointed you
so that you might go and bear fruit
– fruit that will last –
and so that whatever you ask in my name
the Father will give you.

John 15:16

# CONTENTS

A thousand thanks and counting . . .                13

1. Overture to the girl with no name                17

## Foundations for fruitfulness

2. Bananas are not the only fruit                    25
3. A life more fruitful: his invitation              47

## A framework for fruitfulness

4. M1: Modelling godly character                     61
5. M2: Making good work                              79
6. M3: Ministering grace and love                    99
7. M4: Moulding culture                              115
8. M5: Being a Mouthpiece for truth and justice      139
9. M6: Being a Messenger of the gospel               159

## Growing in fruitfulness

10. The gardener's tale                              187

Dedicated to

Ruth Walker and Graeme Macdonald

Pioneers,
Exemplars,
Champions,
Catalysts,
Accompanists,
Hosts,
Friends.

Thank you

# A THOUSAND THANKS
# AND COUNTING ...

Every task – from baking a cake to building a bridge – happens in a context: things are good, things are hard, we've got a cold, a headache, a broken leg, or perhaps an aversion to heights which usually doesn't inhibit cake-making but can be a drawback if you are painting the Forth Bridge. And every task – even the apparently most individualistic – involves other people.

The writing of this book happened during one of the toughest years of my life – that's the context. And the fact that it got written at all is down to the grace of God, and the grace and love and persevering prayers of many, many people – my extraordinary wife, Katriina, my extraordinary family, the team at LICC, and scores of friends. Praise God, I say, for every one of you.

This book began because a pioneering woman in Scotland invited me up to the land of my forefathers to help a group of youngish Scottish workers make a greater impact for Christ in their daily lives. Her name was Ruth Walker. At the time she was a director at Scottish Enterprise and the Chair of

Mission Scotland. Along the way, we all discovered that, if we were to help one another be fruitful where we were, something very different from what we had planned was required. And one of the requirements was to be a bit clearer about what fruitfulness actually looks like on the frontline. And so it was among Chris, Fiona, Frasier, Julie, Marion, Sandra, Sheona, Shona, and Ruth Walker and her deeply astute and ever hospitable husband, Graeme, and Fiona, Gordon and Sarah-Jane from the team at Mission Scotland that the insights began to emerge – invariably over food, invariably with good cheer.

The idea of categorizing aspects of fruitfulness using a number of Ms is entirely due to Beverley Shepherd, who has been a pioneer in workplace ministry for longer than I am permitted to reveal and has taught four Ms of her own for several years. I ended up with six, including three of hers. She, to be fair, is not convinced that you need an extra two, but puts it down to the reality that it always takes me longer to say things than it takes her.

The material has been tested in various forms over the last three years by quite a number of small groups, and we've explored the ideas with scores of church leaders. Indeed, well over 600 people have been involved by now and have offered comments in a variety of ways. Thank you to all of you.

It's also been debated and wrestled with by the LICC team: Charles Hippsley, Neil Hudson, Brian Ladd, Sarah-Jane Marshall, Joe Warton; theologically deepened by Antony Billington; directed and nuanced by Tracy Cotterell; and read so many times by Christine Hughes, my PA, that she could probably sue me for cruelty, if she hadn't read Jesus' caution about taking fellow-believers to court. I've been grateful for the astute comments of Chrissie Ricci and Helen Valler, for the careful guidance and attention to detail of my editor,

Sam Parkinson, and indeed for Kath Stanton's eagle-eyed copyediting.

As for the content, as you will see, there are lots of true stories in this book and therefore lots of people in and through whom God has worked and who have in turn trusted me with their precious testimonies. To every one, thank you. Of course, the stories in the book are not the only ones I've heard. People have told me many more that I haven't been able to include here, which have also shaped my thinking and deepened my sense of wonder at the extraordinary creativity and power of the Lord we serve. Thank you to all of you.

I'm aware too that many, many people have prayed for me and that, without the support of the Friends of LICC and our Board, I would never have been in a position to write this book. I'm very thankful.

I hope it does what you all have been hoping it will do – help many of God's people to be fruitful for him, to his eternal glory.

Mark Greene
LICC
March 2014

. . . we will tell the next generation
the praiseworthy deeds of the LORD,
his power, and the wonders he has done.

Psalm 78:4

# 1.

## OVERTURE TO THE GIRL WITH NO NAME

Last week, the hills were alive with the sound of wheezing.

I was on holiday, walking up Alpine inclines that my breathlessness revealed I really wasn't fit enough to walk up, and then walking down Alpine declines that my groaning thigh muscles revealed I really, really wasn't fit enough to walk down. I stopped a lot – on the plausible but bogus pretext of admiring the spectacular views and recording their glory for future generations. I don't think any of my companions were fooled.

On one of these walks with two much younger, irritatingly fitter men, we fell to asking each other questions: What three books have most influenced you? Schaeffer's *The God Who Is There*, Schluter's *The R Factor*, Mattox's *The Christian Employee*;[1] three favourite hymns or choruses? 'Be Thou My Vision', 'Amazing Grace', 'Praise to the Lord, the Almighty, the King of Creation'; top three (but not the usual suspects) movies? *Crazy Heart*, *The American*, *Cinema Paradiso*; three inspiring people . . . ?

And to that last question I found myself beginning with someone whose story I have probably mulled over more than any other single story in the last fifteen years. I don't know her name, but I do know that she was no more than thirteen years old when the story that will be told for eternity happened. I know that she was living in a war zone and I know that she was a believer in the one true God, the God of Abraham, Isaac and Jacob, the King of the universe, the Shield of David, the Shepherd of Israel, the Lord of Hosts. And I have discovered that her story can help pretty much anyone see their situation differently – bus drivers and business people, housebound carers and travelling sales people, students and retirees . . .

On an ordinary day like any other, an enemy raiding party comes down from the East and does what raiding parties do (2 Kings 5). The girl with no name is captured and ends up as a slave in a pagan household in a pagan land, working for the enemy commander's pagan wife. She is isolated from other believers, wrenched from family and friends, and has nothing but a life of slavery to look forward to. She is just a girl, no more than thirteen years old. And she is in the wrong job, in the wrong place, with the wrong people, with the wrong present and the wrong future. Where, oh where, she must have wondered, is God in all of this? How she must have yearned to be somewhere else.

Now her mistress's husband, Naaman, the enemy commander, the pagan in charge of the army that had raided her town and taken her off into captivity, has leprosy. What is her response to her enemy's illness? Is it to see it as a punishment from God for his idolatry? Is it to wish him a long and painful death? Serves him right – that's what happens to people who mess with God's children. No, her response is recorded in 2 Kings 5:3: 'She said to her mistress, "If only my master would see the prophet who is in Samaria! He would cure him of his leprosy."'

She is not looking to punish her enemy, but to bless him. She doesn't want Naaman dead; she wants him healed. She loves her enemy, long before the greatest King of Israel startled his followers with the injunction to do just that: 'You have heard that it was said, "Love your neighbour and hate your enemy." But I tell you, love your enemies and pray for those who persecute you' (Matthew 5:43–44). Indeed, despite the fact that she has been taken into captivity, despite the fact that her circumstances might lead her to believe that the pagan gods are stronger than the God of Israel, she still believes that her God can do what the pagan gods cannot. And she is right. Furthermore, despite the fact that her God is the God of Abraham, Isaac and Jacob, she believes that her God can and will heal a Gentile, that his grace extends beyond the chosen nation, as indeed God had promised Abraham: 'Through your offspring all nations on earth will be blessed' (Genesis 22:18). And so she utters her one sentence. The consequences are extraordinary.

Naaman is healed of his leprosy. To God be the glory.

Naaman becomes a believer in the one true God. To God be the glory.

Naaman's whole household, the whole army which he commands, the king of Aram whom he serves and his entire court, and the whole nation of Aram learn that the God of Israel can do what the pagan gods cannot. And so, importantly, does the king of Israel and his entire court. To God be the glory.

How has all this come about?

Through one simple, short, love-impelled, faith-soaked sentence uttered by a child. It wasn't much, was it? Just one sentence. But in God's hands how much is a little? How big is

a mustard seed? How valuable a widow's mite? How significant a cup of water?

How has this all come about?

After all, this girl wasn't powerful as the world measures
power. She wasn't highly educated as the world measures education. She was a slave, a child without legal rights,
an enemy in a foreign land, a girl in a patriarchal society. She
was a nobody. We don't even know her name. Around 850
years later the apostle Paul would write:

> Not many of you were wise by human standards; not many
> were influential; not many were of noble birth. But God chose
> the foolish things of the world to shame the wise; God chose the
> weak things of the world to shame the strong. God chose the
> lowly things of this world and the despised things – and the things
> that are not – to nullify the things that are, so that no one may
> boast before him . . . 'Let the one who boasts boast in the Lord.'
> (1 Corinthians 1:26–29, 31)

How has all this come about?

Was not this unnamed servant girl in the wrong job, in the
wrong country, with the wrong people? Mustn't she have
yearned to be elsewhere? Don't we sometimes do the same?
But what if, for now at least, we are right where we are? What
if, for now at least, the people we are with day by day on
our frontline, down our street, in our fitness class, in our
workplace, are the ones God wants us to love and serve?
What if the bit of God's earth that we're in is the bit God
wants us to help tend and steward into burgeoning life? Who
knows how God might work through any of us on our daily
frontlines?

Do we really need to have a high position, or a university
degree, or lots of money, to have a significant impact for God?

There are lots of stories in this book.

They are all true. Some of them may seem quite ordinary. Some of them are almost beyond imagining. They are all about followers of Jesus who have come to see the places and the people they encounter on their frontlines with hearts shaped by God's redemptive priorities.

Some people's names have been changed (asterisked the first time they appear); most have not. Not many of them are famous; not many of them have degrees in theology, or high-status positions in the world or the church. None of them are missionaries in the traditional sense of the word. Their stories are testimonies that the God of Abraham, Isaac and Jacob, of Ruth and Esther, the God of Moses and Elijah, of Mary and Elizabeth, of Peter and Paul, of Lydia and Phoebe, the God of the unnamed servant girl and the Aramean commander works powerfully, wondrously, diversely, mysteriously through his people today.

But this book is not an exhortation to become like any of those people, to become someone you are not, though there is much to learn from them. Rather, it is an encouragement, I hope, to grow more alert to the ways that the God and Father of our Lord Jesus Christ has been working, is working, might work in and through you right where you are, whatever your frontline. After all, we are increasingly hearing about the creative ways that local church congregations are reaching out in mission into neighbourhoods and local communities, about how Christians are sacrificially offering time and energy and talent to support such initiatives, and about the wonderful ways God is working across the nation. Most of us, though, can't realistically be involved in such church-based activities for much more than five hours a week. But what if we were equipped to take the opportunities to be fruitful for God in the other 115 hours that we're awake week by week? What joy might we know in walking with him moment by moment in all we do? What might we see God do? What difference might that make in our needy land?

Indeed, we have seen what happens when God's people work together to make an impact on a local neighbourhood, but we have yet to see what extraordinary things might happen in the offices and factories, cafés and clubs, fields and forests of our land when God's people really work together to support the daily mission of their brothers and sisters where God has placed them. May that day come soon.

This book, then, seeks to do two things: to help us see where we are with fresh eyes, and to explore a range of ways in which we might grow more fruitful for God right where we are.

So, may the Lord work mightily in you on your frontline. May he enable you to support other Christians on theirs, so that the people around us who do not know Jesus might be blessed, healed, strengthened, saved, transformed and released into our Father's service, so that they might declare, like Naaman, 'Now I know that there is no God in all the world except in Israel' (2 Kings 5:15).

That's my prayer. Might it be yours too?

To him be the glory.

## Note

1. Francis A. Schaeffer, *The God Who Is There* (IVP, 1998); Michael Schluter and David Lee, *The R Factor* (Hodder & Stoughton, 1993); Robert Mattox, *The Christian Employee* (Bridge Publishing Inc., 1999).

# FOUNDATIONS FOR FRUITFULNESS

Then God said,
'Let the land produce vegetation:
seed-bearing plants and trees on the land
that bear fruit with seed in it,
according to their various kinds.'
And it was so.

Genesis 1:11

---

This is to my Father's glory,
that you bear much fruit,
showing yourselves to be my disciples.

Jesus, John 15:8

# 2.

# BANANAS ARE NOT
# THE ONLY FRUIT

*Chloë is a student. She's been told that God will use her after she leaves university. She's excited by that prospect. But because she's been told her real mission will be after she leaves, she's not really thinking about how God might work through her now, except in evangelistic conversations.*

*Ed works in a factory. He's bored and he's been praying for a new job for two years. He wants to do something for God – become a worship leader perhaps. Ed thinks his mission is somewhere else. And because he thinks his mission is somewhere else, he's not really been thinking about how he could be fruitful for God where he is.*

*Chris has just turned sixty and is involved in her local church. She's had arthritis for over thirty years – painful, limiting, confidence-sapping – and for a good amount of that time Chris has needed hydrotherapy sessions at the local swimming pool. And she hasn't really been thinking about how God might want to work through her there.*

*One day, pretty much like any other, Chloë discovered that God could work in and through her at university in a rich variety of ways. Yes, in evangelistic conversation, but also in seminars and in writing essays and in sharing a flat and in finding creative ways to help a friend get to the lectures she really needed to get to . . .*

*One day, Ed realized that if God wasn't giving him a new job, he must have something he wanted him to do right where he was . . . and he began to see what that was. He started to get in a bit earlier for his shift, and looked for ways to bless people, befriend people and pray for them. And over time, he saw God working.*

*And one day, Chris realized that she had a frontline, a place of ministry and mission, and it was with the people she met in the hydrotherapy pool, the people she'd got to know over many years, people with whom she had something significant in common, people she actually got into the pool with, people that God had uniquely gifted her to reach . . . Her illness no longer made her a victim; it gave her a ministry.*

Chloë, Ed, Chris – people of different ages in very different circumstances, all wanting to serve God, and all feeling that they didn't have a place to do it, didn't have a frontline. In this chapter, we'll look briefly at what I mean by 'frontline' and then offer an overview of the framework for fruitfulness we'll be exploring.

By 'frontline', I'm primarily meaning a place or a time where we meet fairly regularly with people who don't know Jesus. You may not think you have a frontline like that, but pause a moment: where are the places that you do meet people who don't know Jesus? And which of those might God be calling you to minister in? For one woman, it turned out to be her local Costcutter; for one mum it was the people she meets at the school gate; for one NHS administrator it was the hospital she'd been in for sixteen years; for one retiree it was simply seeing that group of old friends in a fresh way. What's yours?

Of course, most of us are also called to serve among Christians too, some of us in very difficult situations. You may be caring for a housebound child, or a mentally ill spouse, or an older parent. You know it's the place God has for you, hard though it is, and it is almost certainly a context for extraordinary, wondrously God-glorifying fruitfulness, even if not many other people see it.

However, in different ways and in different seasons, all of us have a context where we meet people who don't know Jesus. For some of us, there might be quite a few. And, of course, those places change over time. For example, since I've been writing this book, I've spent quite a lot of time in a local library and got to know some of the staff a bit, and I've found myself praying for one person in particular. Last week, she was serving me a cup of coffee – libraries have to compete with Starbucks these days – and as she did so, I asked her slightly mischievously, 'Have you read any good books recently?' Given my playful tone, I wasn't prepared for her reply: 'Not really. I've only been doing light reading – that's all I can manage at the moment.' And it made me wonder. And pray for whatever pressure, pain or worry has meant that she can only really 'manage light reading' at the moment.

Frontlines change. Yours might be a place where you spend a whole lot of time, or it might be a place you go to only once a week, but you probably already have a context where you engage with people who don't know Jesus, even if you don't think of it that way.

## A door opens

Here's a story that Neil Hudson, one of my colleagues, told me.

Gateshead. Wednesday. Around 8.30 pm.

Isabelle's house, Isabelle's front room, Isabelle's cups and plates and cakes. The home group is meeting. They are thinking about where their individual frontlines might be. They are thinking about where they spend time during their ordinary week with people who don't know Jesus. They've been going round the room and it's Isabelle's turn. She pauses: 'Well, I don't really think I have a frontline. I mean, I'm retired. I look after my husband, I look after the house, I do a few things at church, I see my grandchildren . . . No, I don't really think I have a frontline.'

It's one of those moments that can easily turn to embarrassment. Someone is out of sync with the crowd, like turning up to a party dressed as a pink flamingo, only to discover that it's not a fancy-dress party at all, but a formal civic reception for His Excellency, the Ambassador of Saudi Arabia.

There's a pause because Isabelle doesn't have a frontline – and no-one seems to disagree.

Neil says, 'So, tell us about your grandchildren.'

Isabelle begins and then says, '. . . and the eldest comes round for Sunday lunch three or four times a month. She asks about church and the sermon and so on.'

There's another pause.

'And how old is your grandchild?' Neil asks.

No-one knew it at that moment, but Isabelle's world was about to change. And so was her home group's.

'She's twenty-three.'

The door to a new way of thinking swings wide on its hinges.

She's twenty-three. The room begins to work that through. Pretty much every Sunday, Isabelle is having a significant conversation about church life and biblical teaching with someone who is not a Christian and who is twenty-three . . . right slap bang in the middle of the age group that the church in the UK is finding hardest to reach. And they didn't know.

The group agrees that they'd better start praying for Isabelle.

And the pastor who happens to be there starts to think about how he can include something in his sermons at 11.30 that helps Isabelle with her twenty-three-year-old grand-daughter at 1.30.

And Isabelle realizes that she had a frontline and she hadn't seen it, that God had been working through her and she hadn't seen it. As she put it, 'I didn't think God wanted to work in my family.'

Isabelle hadn't seen it. And nor had her brothers and sisters in Christ. And nor had her pastor. They hadn't seen it because they were looking for ministry opportunities in the wrong places. Isabelle had a frontline right where she was. And it only took a few simple questions about her daily life to reveal it.

At one level, nothing changed in Isabelle's life. But this new realization gave her confidence. It made her intentional about praying. It encouraged her to be looking for signs of God at work. And it made her group intentional about praying for her frontline. It changed the conversations they had with one another, and it made the pastor think differently about his preaching. Quite a result from a two-minute conversation.

Three months later, Neil went back to Gateshead, and Isabelle came up and excitedly told him, 'I'm on a roll now – I'm not only talking to my granddaughter, but my daughter is coming to church.'

And the story, of course, is not finished yet.

This dream of a fruitful life on the frontline isn't a mirage. It's not some lofty theoretical vision of the life less ordinary, attainable only by a tiny cadre of 'super saints' whose knowledge of the Bible has, in the last thousand years, been matched only by William Tyndale, whose prayer life makes a hermit monk's look dilettante, and whose evangelistic prowess has seen no equal since the heydays of Billy Graham. No, over the last thirty years I've seen scores of people living fruitfully on their frontlines, quietly doing extraordinary ordinary things in ordinary places. Often they don't think much of it, don't think that their stories are worth telling anyone because theirs aren't the kind of stories that usually get told in our churches or in our conferences or in our magazines.

So what does fruitfulness look like?

## Bananas are not the only fruit

About four years ago, I did some work with a group of Scots in their twenties and thirties. They did a variety of jobs – a mum, a sales assistant, a graphic designer, a teacher, an actor, a doctor – and they were involved in a variety of churches. Still, they had one thing in common: when it came to their frontline, none of them thought that they were being fruitful. Take Elaine,* for example.

Elaine was a head teacher who had turned round two failing primary schools in a tough area of Glasgow. Now that's an extraordinary achievement. She had transformed the lives of hundreds of children and their families, and indeed the communities they were in. She had brought hope and dignity and joy, and opened up a different future for hundreds of people, but she didn't think she'd done anything for God. And she couldn't see that she had, because, in her mind, fruitfulness had been confined to direct evangelism. If it didn't involve an evangelistic conversation or conversion, it wasn't fruit.

Elaine was not alone either in that group or in the church at large. Vast numbers of Christians don't believe that they are being fruitful for God, because fruitfulness has been narrowly defined as evangelism. Now, if you don't think anything other than evangelism matters to God, then at the end of an average day or an average week at work or at the school gate, it's pretty easy to feel that you aren't doing anything significant for God, that your day, your week has been a bit of a waste. And so, perhaps you conclude that God is not working through you, that maybe you aren't good enough for God to work through, that you are a second-class Christian. And so, it's quite likely that you will feel discouraged or perhaps detached from God's real work in the world.

Furthermore, if you believe that new converts are the only evidence of fruitful living, then you are unlikely to think that anything else is really worth telling other people about, even if you have transformed the lives of hundreds of children and their families. So you don't – and that reinforces the perception that the only thing that really counts to the church and to God is evangelism.

Now evangelism really does matter. In fact, nothing matters more for an individual human being than their relationship with God through Jesus. People need to know the good news of Jesus, and they won't come to know him unless they see him or hear about him. So we are called to pray for the salvation of those who don't know Jesus, to ask God to draw them to himself, to ask God what he wants us to do, to be intentional and persevering and ready to speak and bold and gentle when opportunity arises. But evangelism, as we shall see, is not the only expression of fruitful living, any more than bananas are the only fruit.

Now I happen to love bananas. I love them when they are green and hard, and yellow and firm. And I love them when they are brown and squidgy. I eat them with cereal, in sandwiches, on toast. I eat them mashed with cold milk and a sprinkle of sugar or a filigree of honey. I eat them for breakfast, for a mid-morning pick-me-up, for lunch, for dessert . . . I love bananas. And if you told me that I could only ever have one fruit, it would be bananas, despite my adoration of raspberries and grapes and mangos. But bananas are not the only fruit. In fact, there are quite a lot of things that are fruit that we don't necessarily think of as fruit – tomatoes, for example, and pumpkins. Pumpkins are in fact the biggest fruit, and the largest recorded pumpkin weighed in at 2,032 lb (as of October 2013), the equivalent of approximately 51,209 strawberries. Bananas are not the only fruit, any more than new converts are the only fruit that God is concerned about.

What we need is a richer picture of what fruitfulness in Christ looks like.

## Fruitfulness in the Bible

Biblically, the first mention of human fruitfulness comes in Genesis 1:28 (esv), and it's clearly a reference to having children: 'Be fruitful and multiply.' You'll be relieved to know that I won't be offering any tips on that topic. However, as the Bible unfolds, 'fruit' is also used as an overall metaphor for the consequences of the obedient, godly life. Psalm 1, for example, reads:

> Blessed is the one
>   who does not walk in step with the wicked . . .

but whose delight is in the law of the LORD,
    and who meditates on his law day and night.
That person is like a tree planted by streams of water,
    which yields its fruit in its season,
and whose leaf does not wither –
    whatever they do prospers.
(verses 1–3)

Godly living shaped by godly obedience leads to a life that fulfils the purposes God has for it – fruit at the right time. Psalm 92:12–15 picks up the same theme, but clarifies the lifelong nature of this kind of fruitfulness:

The righteous will flourish like a palm tree,
    they will grow like a cedar of Lebanon.
planted in the house of the LORD,
    they will flourish in the courts of our God.
They will still bear fruit in old age,
    they will stay fresh and green,
proclaiming, 'The LORD is upright.'

Fruitfulness is the result of righteous living, of being planted in the house of God, of having one's roots in God, of being in God. Indeed, in Deuteronomy, there is a direct link between obedience to God's wide-ranging laws and the nation's economic, societal, geopolitical, physical, emotional and relational well-being (Deuteronomy 11:13–25).

The prophet Isaiah explores fruitfulness in a number of ways, as a consequence of personal obedience (3:10), and as a promise of future national redemption (32:15–18). He also uses the symbol of a vineyard to represent Israel (Isaiah 5:1–7). Will Israel be fruitful? Will it be cut down?

Later, in Isaiah 53:11, the fruit of the Messiah's suffering will be the salvation of many souls:

> He will see the light of life and be satisfied;
> by his knowledge my righteous servant will justify many,
>    and he will bear their iniquities.

There are many types of fruitfulness in the Old Testament.

In the New Testament, John the Baptist (Matthew 3:8–10), Jesus and Paul all explore the idea of fruitfulness, and tend to contrast good and bad fruit. All people will produce fruit. The question is what kind? And the kind of fruit they produce is entirely determined by their true character, by who they follow and how closely.

Jesus looks at this most extensively in John 15, where, in the upper room on the night before his death, he characterizes himself as the true vine and the disciples as branches that he wants to see bearing abundant fruit. However, there is a warning: they cannot be fruitful unless they remain in him. And if they don't bear fruit, what use are they? Here, to be in Christ means to obey him, to love him, to lead a life dependent on him, to persevere, to soak in his Word and, vitally, to pray. Fruit is the consequence of prayer in Jesus' name, of a vital, organic, responsive relationship with Christ. Of course, it's not just in chapter 15 that John's Gospel explores fruitfulness. Indeed, later, as Jesus' teaching of the disciples turns into prayer for them (John 17), he makes it clear that he also expects to see other people become his followers through the disciples' message (John 17:20). There are many types of fruit.

Similarly, in his letters, Paul sets out various lists of character qualities that please God, that are the direct result of the work of his Spirit in a believer's life. In Galatians 5:22–23 he characterizes such qualities as the fruit of the Spirit.

In sum, good fruit is any attitude, any word, any action that pleases God. Fruit is any consequence that is in line with his will – an animal properly cared for, a local pond cleaned up, a person saved, healed, fed, given a cup of water, taught, corrected, trained in righteousness, defended, rescued from injustice, or loved in any godly way. Fruit is anything done with authentic love. Indeed, there is no evidence that one type of fruit is more important to God than another, no evidence of a 'fructal hierarchy', as if speaking up for justice might be more important than modelling godly character, or making good work more important than moulding culture. Similarly, there is no evidence that evangelists receive a greater reward in heaven than those who ploughed the ground or those who sowed the seed. It is God who gives life (1 Corinthians 3:6).

Ultimately, then, fruit is anything that brings glory to God. Here is the apostle Peter:

> Live such good lives among the pagans that, though they accuse
> you of doing wrong, they may see your good deeds and glorify
> God on the day he visits us.
> (1 Peter 2:12)

In other words, the people we work with, live next to, play Nintendo with may or may not respond to God in our lifetime, or even theirs, but that isn't the only time the impact of our faithful living gets measured. It gets measured on the day of judgment. Peter has an eternal perspective. A life well lived in Christ will redound to God's glory on the day he returns. On that day, even those who have rejected God will acknowledge that God is great, that God is God, that he is worthy. On that day, they will acknowledge that they saw the transformative power of God in his people's lives.

It isn't that God is not interested in people acknowledging him in time. Jesus makes it clear that he is: 'In the same way, let your light shine before others, that they may see your good deeds and glorify your Father in heaven' (Matthew 5:16). However, 'now' is not the only criterion.

Similarly, it's not that the apostle Peter isn't interested in evangelism or healing or serving the poor or raising the dead. In Acts 2, Peter preaches the first evangelistic sermon, and over 3,000 people respond. In Acts 3, Peter and John heal a crippled beggar. In Acts 6, as the number of believers grows, Peter and the other apostles ensure the distribution of food to the poor among them. In Acts 9, we read that Peter raises a woman from the dead. All of that is good, but its eternal value is not because 3,000 are saved or because a woman is raised from the dead; its eternal value is that it brings glory to God. We live to glorify God. And God is glorified as his character, his priorities, his goodness and indeed his power are expressed through our everyday lives. The goal of fruit-fulness is to bring glory to God.

## Fruit, glorious fruit

In John's Gospel, Jesus puts it this way: 'This is to my Father's glory, that you bear much fruit, showing yourselves to be my disciples' (John 15:8).

Jesus wants the disciples to be fruitful to the glory of the Father, just as his own life and death were intended to be. Indeed, it is precisely because of his obedient life and death that:

> Therefore God exalted him [Jesus] to the highest place
>    and gave him the name that is above every name,

> that at the name of Jesus every knee should bow,
> in heaven and on earth and under the earth,
> and every tongue acknowledge that Jesus Christ is Lord,
> *to the glory of God the Father.*
> (Philippians 2:9–11, italics mine)

Ultimately, Jesus' death on the cross is intended to bring glory to the Father. So are our lives.

Of course, that can sound as if God is rather vain, as if he is fame-starved. However, God's desire is that we know him for who he really is. So, the goal of all that we do is that others see God for who he truly is. And God's splendour is glimpsed not only through his acts of sovereign power and grace, but through how he works in and through us. When Moses had been in the presence of the Lord, his face shone. So, as we live in step with the Spirit, God's glory radiates out through who we are in him, what we do and say in his power, like light beaming from the facets of a diamond. The point here is that fruitfulness is not an end in itself. Fruitfulness is intended to point to the wonder of the Father.

Everything we do is intended to bring glory to the Father. We may, for example, give our money to the Lord, some a million, some a mite, but who brings more glory to God? The poor widow whom Jesus points out to his disciples in the Jerusalem temple or the generous, very wealthy tax collector he publicly honours in Jericho (Luke 21:1–4; 19:1–10)? God isn't interested in numbers alone. Many received Jesus when Peter spoke (Acts 2), and few did when Stephen spoke (Acts 7), but God was glorified on both occasions.

In sum, there are many types of fruitfulness in the New Testament, and their ultimate goal is to bring glory to God.

## A framework for fruitfulness

This book seeks to stir our imaginations about how we might be fruitful to God's glory. But what will help us see the possibilities? Well, in the group I worked with in Scotland, we found that we needed a simple framework to come back to, something to remind ourselves of the big picture, to help us reflect on what God might have been doing already and to get us thinking about how we might be fruitful in the future. And so, we developed what we've now ended up calling the '6Ms'. They've proved helpful. Here they are.

On your frontline, how might you:

M1: Model godly character?
M2: Make good work?
M3: Minister grace and love?
M4: Mould culture?
M5: Be a Mouthpiece for truth and justice?
M6: Be a Messenger of the gospel?

Of course, this set of questions isn't comprehensive, but it covers quite a lot of biblical ground. It includes our attitudes and our actions, our work and our words. It includes a concern for the individuals we meet and for the organizations, families and nations we are part of – the culture we are in. It includes a concern for personal salvation and for global issues of justice. And it's a framework that can be embraced by apprentices and retirees, kids and stay-at-home parents, office workers and people who are unemployed. In fact, it applies whether the context is brimming with people who already know God or a context where no-one apart from you does. Yes, this book is focused on frontlines where there are non-believers, but fruitfulness for Christ is not confined to those contexts.

After all, wherever we are, we all get to try to *model godly character*, try to display the fruit of the Spirit in whatever idyllic or grim circumstances we find ourselves. What do love, joy, peace, patience, kindness, goodness, faithfulness, gentleness and self-control look like where you are (Galatians 5:22–23)?

And we all have work to do, whether or not we are paid for it: dishes to wash, shirts to iron, shopping to do, essays to write, calls to make, deals to do. We all have an opportunity to *make good work*. What difference might it make if we committed our ordinary daily tasks to God, asked him for help, consciously did it for his glory?

We all get to *minister grace and love* to people: offering a nugget of advice, looking out for a colleague, caring about the checkout person, taking an initiative on someone else's behalf, going beyond what we have to. Even if we are housebound and living alone, there are still opportunities to extend grace to the people who come to our door, the people who call us up . . . And that's fruit.

We all have an opportunity to *mould the culture* of the places we're in: the way we do things in our family, our form at school, our team, the hall of residence, the office, the church. And when we contribute to moulding a culture which better reflects God's ways, which better expresses the priorities of his kingdom, that's fruit.

At some point, too, we will all probably have an opportunity to *be a mouthpiece for truth and justice*, whether for ourselves or for another – with the local council, with a boss, or a classmate who's been unjustly accused: 'It wasn't him, Miss.' God loves justice. And loves to see it done.

And by God's grace and in his time, we all have opportunities to *be a messenger of the gospel*, to communicate the reason for the hope that we have in Jesus, to bring a biblical

perspective to a conversation, or just to tell others the difference Jesus has made, is making, in our lives.

Of course, we often get to display more than one type
of fruit at the same time. Sometimes you can look at the
same story through the lens of each of the Ms and see
evidence of fruitfulness. Indeed, the 6Ms can be likened
to a six-sided hollow perspex cube: pop a situation into the
cube and look at it from those six angles. Take Peter, for
example.

### Rubbish calling?

After living for twenty-five years in the same place, Peter
retired and moved to a town where he didn't know anyone.
He didn't have an obvious frontline, though there were a lot
of things Peter could do, including preaching and teaching
and counselling. He prayed and asked God, 'What do you
want me to do?'

It is a brave prayer. And a humble one. You might not get
an answer you like.

For Peter, the Lord brought Jeremiah 29:7 to mind: 'Seek
the peace and prosperity of the city to which I have carried
you into exile.' And Peter wondered, 'How can I bless the town
God has brought me to?' So he prayed again. And the Lord
told him to pick up litter.

It reminded him of Jesus washing the disciples' feet in the
upper room – cleaning off the dirt. So he went to the council
and asked them for a litter-picking claw, and they gave him
one on 'permanent loan'. And so it came to pass that on
the days when Peter went on his two-mile walk to, through
and from the nature reserve close to his home, he'd pray and
praise God for his world and pick up the litter that marred it
and put it in a plastic bag. And he'd smile at people he passed
on the path and say 'hello'.

Pretty soon people started to say 'hello' back, and little conversations began. And the months passed, and people would ask, 'Why do you do it?' 'Because God loves the world he has made.' Or they would enquire: 'Are you being paid?' He hasn't been, of course. And one person said, 'That's a thankless job. You'll get to heaven for that.' So Peter replied that he hoped to get to heaven not because he picked up the litter, but because he knows Jesus who gave his life for him. During Easter week, he says 'hello' to the people he normally says 'hello' to and gives them a gift – a little cross, made, he tells them, from olive wood from Israel where Jesus lived, a gift to remind us that at Easter Jesus died and rose again. And some people have indeed come to evangelistic meetings at the church.

So, as he walks, Peter the litter-picker picks up litter. And drivers he doesn't know toot their horns and wave in respect and gratitude. And then, on one ordinary day like any other ordinary day, a white van pulled up beside him. The window rolled down, and the man in the white van who had, of course, somewhere to go, and work to do, said, 'Thanks very much'.

Well, I wonder what strikes you about that story? In what ways has Peter been fruitful on his frontline?

Peter has modelled godly character, displaying kindness and no doubt some self-control and patience as he picks up litter that is the result of other people's lack of self-control and patience and selflessness. M1.

He has made good work, cleaning up the park. M2.

He has taken the initiative to minister to strangers with grace and love. M3.

He has moulded the culture of the walking community in the nature reserve – it's a friendlier place. M4.

He has been a mouthpiece for the truth about God's concern for creation and for the right ways of stewarding it. M5.

And Peter has been a messenger of the gospel, telling others about why he does what he does, about his own relationship with Jesus, and inviting people to find out more in a church context. M6.

And all Peter was doing was picking up litter.

There are lots of ways to be fruitful for God. And all these Ms work together: modelling godly character creates better soil for godly testimony; working hard to make other people's lives better confirms that the gospel is about joy in this life as well as in the next; serving others lovingly and graciously makes the message of a loving, gracious Servant-King much more compelling; taking a risk to stand up against injustice makes the claim that God cares about injustice much more persuasive. So it is that our lives in Christ reinforce our words about Christ. And our words about Jesus help others to see that it is Jesus who has transformed our lives and can transform theirs too.

Furthermore, as we become better at seeing God working in and through us in these various ways, as we see him answering prayer, we have more to say about God's living love to the people we meet on our frontline. 'God did that', 'God helped me with this' . . . It enriches our evangelism.

Of course, these kinds of models can become oppressive. 'Now I don't just get to feel guilty about evangelism and my woeful failure to crowbar a gospel presentation into a casual conversation about the weather. Now I've got to be a 6M disciple . . . Oh Lord . . .'

No.

These six Ms aren't another set of holy 'to-dos' to add to our already-too-long list of boxes to tick.

These are lenses to help us spot how God might already be working in us.

And they are snapshots of what kingdom living might look

like, snapshots to help us see what God might do in and through us on our frontlines.

They are there to spark our imagination and spur our prayers for ourselves and for one another. What might God want you to focus on to begin with? It might surprise you. It probably surprised Peter – he might have expected something else, given that he had actually spent thirty-five years working as an ordained minister of the Church of England. A humble man.

In Peter's case, God prompted him to seek 'the peace and prosperity' of the place to which he had called him. Interestingly, the words 'peace and prosperity' in Jeremiah 29:7 are a translation of a single Hebrew word, 'shalom'. To pray for shalom is to pray for divine blessing on every aspect of our existence – our physical well-being, our emotional, mental and spiritual well-being, our economic, ecological, political and social well-being. Praying for shalom means praying for things to be as God intends – whole, complete, beautiful, fulfilled. Still, within that huge overall goal, God called Peter to begin with a particular act in a particular part of his world – pick up litter in the park. When Peter began, he could not have known what it might lead to. How could he? But humble obedience to our Lord is fruit that pleases the Lord – he sees it as love (John 14:21). And if, in the end, the only result was that litter was picked up, would that have been good? Yes, it would. Peter might have yearned for more, but it would have been good and God-pleasing.

Indeed, before we explore the Ms and their implications for your frontline in more detail, it is vital to see that these 6Ms are all an intrinsic part of what it means to follow Jesus day by day, and, amazing and sobering and humbling as it is, they all contribute to his glorious purposes in time and eternity.

## A prayer for this moment

Father,
give me eyes and heart to see
where you would have me serve you,
the desire and courage to ask
what you would have me do,
and the love and grace
to do it.
For your joy and glory may it be.
Amen

## Questions for prayerful reflection

Where is your frontline? In what ways have you already seen God working in and through you there? What are its particular challenges?

Close your eyes and prayerfully imagine Jesus meeting you on your frontline and walking around with you. What does he point out to you?

Which of the Ms do you feel you are strongest in? Which M has most room for growth? Do you think your best Christian friend would agree with your assessment?

Renewal & restoration

For
God
was pleased
to have all his fulness dwell in him,
and through him to reconcile to himself
all things,
whether
things
on earth
or things
in heaven,
by making
peace
through
his
blood,
shed
on
the
cross.

Colossians 1:19–20

# 3.
## A LIFE MORE FRUITFUL:
## HIS INVITATION

In a primary school close to where the A404 runs down by a great oak, there was a group of Christian children. Every year, the whole school – the teachers, staff and kids – discuss what the school's values should be, the values that are displayed in the school hall on paper elephant heads and shape all that everyone does. Anyone may suggest a new value to replace an existing value, and every year everyone votes.

The school, which is called Holy Trinity, is a Church of England school, but counts among its people Muslims, Hindus, Sikhs and many with no particular faith at all.

And so the group of Christian children pondered how they might, in this place of study and play, of talk and food and many faiths, bring the light of Christ to shine. And so they went to the head teacher and said, 'We think one of our values should be "What would Jesus do?"'

And so the head talked to the Muslims, who didn't mind because Jesus is a prophet, after all. And she talked to the Hindus and, after *much discussion among themselves and with the Christian children, the Hindu children said, 'This is a Christian school, after all, so we feel you have every right to have this value.' And then the whole school voted, and 'What would Jesus do?' became one of the school's values, one of the criteria by which everything that happens in that school would be evaluated. And Jesus' name was raised and lifted up – literally – on a paper elephant head on the walls of a primary school hall. Glory indeed to God.*

Now those Christian children had almost certainly never heard grown-up phrases like 'moulding culture' (M4) or 'transforming ethos', but that is precisely what they had done.

And they were ten years old.

Of course, their achievement might not seem very significant to you. They didn't change the national education system, they didn't see a wave of conversions, but they had an impact for God on every child and adult in their school. They did something that was in line with God's purposes, with his mission.

It is something we are all called to – to live our lives in line with God's bigger purposes. Indeed, the clearer we are about his bigger purposes, the easier it is to see why our character and daily actions and words are important, and how they can contribute to those purposes.

## A bigger mission

In the first chapter of his letter to the Christians in Colossae, Paul summarizes the scope of God's purposes. He begins by expressing gratitude for the fruitfulness of the believers in Colossae, a fruitfulness that is part of a global movement of the gospel. He goes on to pray that their fruitfulness would increase as they follow Christ and he then sets their lives in the context of God's overarching plan, a plan that finds expression in creation. Jesus, Paul declares, is the image of the invisible God, the firstborn over all creation, the Creator of all things: 'For in him all things were created: things in heaven and on earth, visible and invisible, whether thrones or powers or rulers or authorities' (verse 16).

All things. Things visible to the naked eye – toucans, elephants, bananas – and things invisible to the naked eye – electricity, sound waves, Higgs bosons. Then Paul succinctly summarizes Jesus' engagement in the universe: 'all things have been created through him and for him' (verse 16).

As such, Paul gives us two main reasons for Jesus' interest in 'all things':

1. He created them
2. He created them for himself

In other words, Jesus is not like a carpenter who makes a chair and sells it to someone who can then do whatever they like with it. No, Jesus makes the chair and it remains his, even if he expects others to use it – sit on it, stand on it, fend off lions with it – and look after it – dust it, wash it, and polish it to a rich and radiant sheen with cedar oil and beeswax. It's his.

So, if 'all things' – from a great blue whale to a 0.139 mm fairy fly, from mountain granite to ocean coral, from an individual to the government of the United Kingdom – if all were created *by* and *for* Christ, it is very, very difficult to see why he would not be interested in how we steward and shape it. If all creation, visible and invisible, is his, wouldn't he be interested in the impact that our activities in the kitchen, at school, in factories, fields and offices, in government and radio stations and art galleries and hospitals and science labs have on his creation and on people created in his image?

And he is.

Indeed, Jesus is so concerned for 'all things' that he set aside his majesty and humbled himself to come to earth as a baby, as a carpenter's son. And he came not only to give his life as a ransom for many, but, as Paul goes on to write: 'to reconcile to himself all things, whether things on earth or things in heaven, by making peace through his blood, shed on the cross' (Colossians 1:20).

Jesus' sacrifice is not only intended to offer every human being the opportunity for reconciliation with him, but to reconcile all things, all matter, the entire cosmos to himself. Jesus' work on the cross serves to begin to bring all things back into proper relationship with him, to see everything functioning in the way it is meant to. Indeed, he teaches us to pray: 'Your kingdom come, your will be done on earth as it is in heaven.' In other words, Jesus commands us to pray that everything on earth would be as he wants it to be. And he expects us not only to pray those words, and to live in a way that is consistent with them, but to seek to make them a reality. As believers, then, we are part of a divinely ordained movement to change the world. And as believers, we are part of that plan – whatever we do, wherever we are and whatever our age.

## In my ballet class as in heaven?

When my daughter Anna-Marie was younger, we used to read a Bible story and pray before she went to sleep. And quite often, as you might expect, we'd pray the Lord's Prayer. And then one evening, when she was about nine, I suddenly began to wonder what some of these oh-so-familiar, oh-so-rich words might mean to a little girl of nine: 'Your kingdom come, your will be done on earth as it is in heaven.'

It is a prayer that is global in its scope: that God's will would be done on earth as God's will is done in heaven. It's a prayer that says your will be done in my church and in the local council, in the cell group and in the swimming pool, in the Sunday school and in the school, in the soup kitchen and in the hospital, in the factory and the queue for the checkout . . . Nothing is left out.

But what could these words mean to my nine-year-old daughter?

Not very much, I concluded.

So from time to time, we'd pray it differently: 'Your kingdom come, your will be done in my school as in heaven, in my classroom as in heaven, in my ballet class . . .'

Your will be done on earth as it is in heaven and in the bit of the earth you've placed me in, in my street, in my town, on my frontline.

God teaches us to pray this prayer and to live in ways that contribute to its fulfilment – wherever we are.

## Our role in the new era

Often, we tend to focus on the implications of Jesus' sacrifice for personal salvation, but, as we have seen, Paul affirms God's concern for 'all things', God's comprehensive plan for the restoration and redemption of the whole sin-marred universe.

Indeed, the word we translate as 'gospel' comes from the Greek word *euangelion*. In the time of Jesus, it was most used for the celebratory announcement of the victory of a general in battle. In essence, the gospel is not only a message of

salvation for individual souls; it is the announcement of God's
definitive cosmic victory over sin, death and the devil: VU Day
– Victory in the Universe Day. It is the inauguration of a new
era in human history, the beginning of God's kingdom reign,
in which a new relationship with God becomes possible, new
resources of divine wisdom and power become available, and
new possibilities abound in every sphere of life: the blind see,
the lame walk, the dead are raised and the poor are informed
that a new world order has begun. In such a world, nothing
need be the same again. New rules apply.

## The invitation

The invitation to follow Jesus, then, is not just an invitation to spend eternity in his presence, not just an invitation
to others to spend eternity in his presence; it is an invitation to cooperate with him in making his world as much
like he intends it to be before he returns. That's his invitation
to you.

Which frankly sounds like something worth giving one's
life to.

Yes, that sounds very grand, but it is worked out day by day
in our ordinary lives, whether we are, like the Colossians,
living in a smallish town in Asia Minor, or a bustling city in
the Midlands of England.

Furthermore, because we know God is interested in
whatever we do, because we are not called to part-time
discipleship or evenings and weekends discipleship but
whole-life discipleship, we can be confident that God is with
us in everything. And that means we can talk to him about
everything, seek his wisdom and resources for everything,
rely on him in everything.

God is not like some stern, furrow-browed father who is only concerned about his daughter's academic results and couldn't care less about her interest in nice clothes or her inexplicable penchant for a sitcom like *How I Met Your Mother* or her love of salt and vinegar *Squares*. No, God is interested in the whole shebang. There are few gifts more joyous than a friend about whom you can say, 'We can talk about anything.' Well, we've all got one. And he is constantly available.

So, we are all called to participate in God's grand mission – nothing less than the renewal and regeneration of his universe. And everything we do now has the capacity to do that. An act of generosity, for example, is not only a beautiful thing in itself; it is a foretaste of the kingdom where abundance flows and there is no lack.

## Of grand designs and a man called Bill

Recently I went down to visit a couple who lived on some land with a number of burnt-out oast houses that had been abandoned so long ago that a twenty-foot tree was flourishing in the middle of one of them. They decided to convert the houses into a Christian retreat centre in such a way that people who are used to fine things would feel comfortable and people who are not used to fine things would feel at ease, honoured, treated. In sum, they'd not only redeemed a ruin, but had sought to create a place where anyone, rich or poor, old or young, might be refreshed in body and spirit, and know the presence of God and come closer to him. It's a beautiful place – a grand design for a glorious purpose. And it is also a foretaste of the way things will one day be, the first fruits that point to a greater and more wondrous reality – of the place where all, poor and rich, will rejoice at the wedding banquet of the Son of God and exult in the presence of Father, Son and Holy Spirit. Of course, creating a retreat centre was a big venture, but, as we accept God's invitation to participate in his purposes day by day, all our actions, words, attitudes can be signs of his kingdom now and foretastes of his kingdom to come.

When I was a student doing theology, I asked one of my lecturers who the most influential person in his Christian life was. The lecturer was Dr Harold Rowdon, and his field was church history, so he'd read about a lot of Christian men and women across the centuries. He'd also taught at the London School of Theology for about thirty-nine years, so he'd met a huge number of godly theologians, missionaries, pastors, preachers, social activists . . . He had a legion of luminaries to choose from.

But he didn't hesitate.

'Oh,' he said, 'there was someone in my church growing up – there was just something holy about him.'

He didn't mention his name at the time. But a few years later I asked him:

'Bill Sparks'.

It is no small thing to radiate the holiness of Christ, no small thing to walk through this world as a pointer to the radiant holiness that all those who follow him will one day experience in his presence in the company of the saints.

To God be the glory.

In sum, every Christian has a part to play in God's mission which is nothing less than the renewal and restoration of the entire cosmos. And within that common but high calling, there are many ways to be fruitful to the glory of God, many ways you probably already are fruitful, and many ways you may grow in fruitfulness on your frontline. Sister Wendy

Beckett put it beautifully on *Desert Island Discs* when Kirsty Young asked her:

'When did you first decide you wanted to be a nun?'

'I was a baby,' she replied. 'It was the only thing I wanted because I didn't know there were other ways to love God completely. I now know of course, you know, that you can be a bus conductress or a television person and love God completely.'

## A rough guide to the journey ahead

Indeed, the Ms are a way to explore how you might express your love for God with all your heart and mind and strength. But they aren't intended to be a checklist, some holy highway to God's approval and love. It is by grace, not our efforts or activities, that we are saved.

As you read, you may well find that there are one or two of the Ms to which God draws your particular attention at this time. Indeed, it's unlikely that he would expect any of us to address every aspect of our potential fruitfulness all at once. Equally, it's important to gain a sense of the big picture, of what he may lead you to in the future. Besides, the Ms can't be neatly separated from each other. They are organically connected. Growth in godly character is likely to lead to acts of love and grace. Acts of love and grace may well lead to an opportunity to talk about the love and grace that Jesus has shown you. Being a mouthpiece for truth and justice in your context might well lead to a different kind of culture emerging. Indeed, in any situation, we may have the opportunity to display more than one type of fruitfulness.

There is much to learn about all the Ms – people have written whole books on each of them – though not usually with a focus on the frontline. So I haven't tried to be exhaustive, but I have sought to open up the terrain of each M, highlight some key landmarks and then, at the end of the chapters, suggest some resources that might take you further.

I also haven't tried to offer a story of fruitfulness for every M for every possible frontline – there are too many. However, although frontlines are all different, there are often underlying commonalities in other people's stories that can help us in ours. Peter the litter-picker, for example, was retired and his frontline was a nature reserve, but he was actually inspired to 'walk' in a new way by the story of a young research scientist walking the corridors of a large pharmaceutical company. So, the question Peter's story might raise for us is not: 'Do I have a park to walk in?', but rather, 'Where do I walk?' Or perhaps, 'When I walk, who and what do I see?'

So the stories of other people's actions are obviously not there for you to copy, but rather to stir your imagination and creativity. I don't suppose, for example, that the most effective way to get people in your office to think about the contribution that Jesus could make to corporate culture is to put up WWJD posters in the corridors. But wasn't it a brilliant idea in that school? What might you do?

Ultimately, these Ms are all expressions of the life of Jesus working in you. Godly character, godly work, Spirit-empowered love, potent gospel witness all come from Jesus. Fruitfulness is from Christ. He is the vine; we are the branches. And a severed branch bears no fruit. We can do nothing without him (see John 15:5).

Whatever the fruit, they all have a hint of grape about them.

So, as you explore the Ms with your frontline in mind, approach it prayerfully. What is Jesus saying to you? What stirs you? What makes you afraid or causes you to react with disbelief? What seems impossible or just trivial? You might, like Peter, ask the Lord directly: 'What do you want me to do?' You can trust him not to overwhelm you. And you can also trust him to want to help you grow. He is at work in you, but he does not need you to be perfect in order to work through you. You aren't anyway, and he has more than enough perfection of his own. No, he doesn't need you to be perfect or perfectly ready, but readily available.

God asks us to be willing to take the next step – with him. He may, as he did with Moses, reveal a big, extraordinarily ambitious plan for your frontline, or he may simply prompt you to do something small that may lead to extraordinary things. Or God may prompt you to something the ultimate significance of which you may never know – in your earthly lifetime at least. In his hands, even seeming failure can yield an extraordinary harvest of glory to his name. Just look at the cross.

Still, we don't just read for ourselves. We are all members of God's family. So, as you read, you might ask yourself, what is God saying that he wants me to pass on to someone else? Who is God prompting me to encourage? And, equally, who should I be asking to encourage me in my growing in fruitfulness? *encourage –*

## A prayer for this moment

Our Father in heaven,
hallowed be your name.
Your kingdom come,
your will be done on earth
as it is in heaven.
Your kingdom come,

your will be done in my heart,
my life, my town, my home,
my relationships, my work,
as it is in heaven.
And to your glory may it be.
Amen

## Questions for reflection

*7* Who has been the most influential Christian in your life?
What particular qualities are you especially grateful for?

As you consider your frontline, what in particular do you
think would contribute to its shalom, its peace and prosperity?
And the shalom, the peace and prosperity of the people there?

## Exploring further

Scott D. Allen, *Beyond the Sacred-Secular Divide: A Call to
   Wholistic Life and Ministry* (Seattle: YWAM Publishing,
   2011).
Antony Billington with Margaret Killingray and Helen
   Parry, *Whole Life, Whole Bible: 50 Readings on Living in the
   Light of Scripture* (Abingdon: BRF, 2012).
Julian Hardyman, *Maximum Life: All for the Glory of God*
   (Nottingham: IVP, 2009).
Darrow L. Miller with Marit Newton, *LifeWork: A Biblical
   Theology for What You Do Every Day* (Seattle: YWAM
   Publishing, 2009).
Vaughan Roberts, *God's Big Picture: Tracing the Storyline of
   the Bible* (Nottingham: IVP, 2009).

# A FRAMEWORK FOR
# FRUITFULNESS

I
am
the
vine;
you are the branches.
If you remain in
me
and
I
in you,
you will bear much fruit;
apart from
me
you can do
nothing.

John 15:5

It's tough to argue with someone who has lived so well.

President Bill Clinton on Mother Teresa

# 4.

## M1: MODELLING GODLY CHARACTER

*I hadn't thought about Robert for a while. Robert who was gentle, kind, quietly elegant, rather good at what he did. My PA Robert who contracted a degenerative disease that slowly robbed him of his ability to communicate. And died. He was twenty-six. But today, on the day when I am about to write a chapter on godly character, I get a Facebook message out of the wide blue ether from a former colleague, a friend of his too — Sue, tall, with that rich voice and lofty heels and acute insight. In my mind, she and Robert are inextricably linked, not because they were ever romantically involved, but because I know she admired him so, loved him really, flew from Paris to America to say goodbye. And so I am reminded of Robert's serenity under pressure, his unembittered fortitude in the face of disappointment, his grace when he didn't get the promotion that we all so wanted for him and that he so deserved, the way that his dying young meant he didn't get to find a space to explore and express some of his talents, the way he was able to say to the doctors, 'No heroic measures', not grasping onto life . . .*

*Robert. Gentle. Kind. Noble is probably the word. And I don't know the thousandth of it.*

*Twenty years after his death and I'm writing this with tears in my eyes. Twenty years later and I am still in awe, still grateful. And so I am in no doubt that character speaks, that character makes a difference. In the big things and in the little things. Because it wasn't Robert's dying that brought out his essential character – we'd already seen it in a host of ways. No, it wasn't Robert's dying that brought out his character, but his dying made us stop and recognize how extraordinary it was. To God be the glory.*

I don't suppose many of us have ever even begun to think of ourselves as modelling godly character, never mind being the kind of person people might look at and say, 'Now that's godliness.' But the curious thing is that we might well have thought it about other people. I often do. I often find myself meeting people and thinking, oh, my goodness, look how a particular facet of Christ shines through in their lives – Ana's wondrously gracious ability to create a safe space for people, Kim's steady perseverance in doing all he can to see other people's potential liberated, Tracy's patience.

Character, of course, is not the same as personality. Indeed, it's interesting that in the New Testament we have hardly any explicit descriptions of anyone's personality. We don't know if Thomas was dour, Epaphroditus funny, or Elizabeth shy, but we do know that Thomas was courageous, Epaphroditus persevering and Elizabeth upright. We don't know if Mary, Martha's sister, was a mischievous, playful little pixie of a woman who skipped into the room where Jesus was teaching the male disciples and sat down at the front with a little conspiratorial wink up at Jesus, but we know she was wise. We don't know very much about people's personalities, but we do know that almost all of the New Testament writers are concerned about character, about qualities that have nothing to do with whether we are playful or serious, extrovert or introvert, but rather with the extent to which our faith, hope and love lead to the kind of character that responds appropriately to God, circumstances and others.

## Not just Mr Nice Guy

Godly character isn't just about being nice, about hovering through life with some serene, beatific grin on our faces. Jesus wasn't always 'nice' and things were rarely easy. Jesus is, after all, not just the one who allows himself to be pinned to the cross; Jesus is the one who courageously sets his face to go up to Jerusalem knowing what awaits him. He is the one who calmly makes himself a whip to throw the money changers out of the temple; the one who calls the Pharisees a brood of vipers, and whitewashed tombs; the one who deliberately antagonizes his own home town by making a messianic claim; the one who shocks the establishment by eating and drinking with tax collectors and sinners and letting a prostitute wash his road-dirtied feet with her glorious hair; the one who rebukes his dinner host for not treating him properly. Jesus is not always 'nice' as we might define it. Faithfulness to his mission, obedience to his Father, and love for the people he encountered, demanded more.

Certainly, godly character will often lead to loving actions – and should. But here the emphasis is on 'modelling', on the way we come across to others, on how our character leads people to expect certain kinds of responses from us. 'I wouldn't go in there today; she's in one of her moods.' 'Oh, don't worry, he'll shout, he'll scream, he'll pull your finger-nails out, but he won't kill you . . .'

A few years back, I found myself at the leaving party for Chua Wee Hian, the retiring General Secretary of a global student organization that had seen a host of different challenges over the years – organizational challenges as it grew, financial, theological, missiological challenges, as well as challenges of persecution by governments and university authorities . . . Much wisdom had been required. Mr Chua, said one of his closest colleagues, was 'like a catcher in baseball [the equivalent of a wicketkeeper in cricket] – however hard you throw the ball at him, it always comes back gently.' Character is the qualities in us that lead to the expectation of a particular kind of response – whatever the pressure.

## Spirited living

Modelling godly character is letting the life of Christ flow in and through us. It is about exhibiting the fruit of the Spirit in tough times as well as in easy times. Indeed, the fruit of the Spirit Paul writes about in Galatians 5 is a daunting list, particularly if we remember that Paul was writing to people who were for the most part poor – people without the health service, most of whose children would die before the age of five, people who were under the social pressure that comes from following such a different path from pretty much everyone else. That was then. And of course in some parts of the world much of it still applies. But, whatever our situation, living out love, joy, peace, patience, kindness, goodness, faithfulness, gentleness and self-control on our frontlines is pretty daunting.

It cannot be easy to live out the fruit of the Spirit if you are Richard,* at home with Jean,* who has been suffering from dementia for four years now. And not getting better, of course, just slowly worse, slowly less able to do the things she has been able to do for herself since she was three – eat neatly, go to the loo, walk from A to B – less and less able to remember what she said just a moment ago and the moment before that and the moment before that. Oh, it is not easy on the frontline of caring, day in, night in – and not many days out or nights out – not easy to show love, joy, peace, patience, kindness, goodness, faithfulness, gentleness and self-control in the midst of the daily grieving and the deepening fatigue and the increasing isolation.

Maybe your frontline isn't as demanding as that, but still, I wonder, how high would you mark yourself at the end of an average day on a list like love, joy, peace, patience, kindness, goodness, faithfulness, gentleness and self-control?

Often, perhaps not very highly. Perhaps rightly, perhaps wrongly.

## Louise and the ogre

Louise worked for an ogre. She was PA to probably the most unreasonable boss in Buckinghamshire. He was bad-tempered, temperamental, indifferent to others, changeable. And she worked for the ogre for three years, prayed for strength, prayed that he would change, and prayed that he would become a follower of Jesus. But he didn't. And she felt like an abject failure. In the end, she decided that she couldn't take it any more and she left, feeling like she'd let God down.

A few weeks later, she got a phone call from the woman who had replaced her: 'He is impossible. I've been here three weeks and I'm already thinking of leaving. So I talked to a couple of people and they told me to give you a call. They said you'd done a fantastic job, that you'd always been gracious and upbeat, despite his impossible ways. How did you do it?'

How did she do it?

Well, first of all, she didn't realize that she'd done anything at all. She thought she'd failed. Often *we* don't think that we've done anything much to write about either. We're just living our lives as best we can. And then someone tells us, 'You were so kind, so patient, so self-controlled when everyone else was losing their heads, when it looked as if we were going down.' And perhaps we don't think much of it: 'Well, I suppose, but it's just what I do. I mean, there's nothing remarkable in that.' We're like dolphins being told that we're good at swimming. It doesn't seem very remarkable, unless of course you are a lobster, or a seahorse, or a kangaroo.

The truth is that, when we received Jesus, we became different creations, we were born again. As Paul puts it, 'Therefore, if anyone is in Christ, the new creation has come: the old has gone, the new is here!' (2 Corinthians 5:17).

I take this at face value. I was a caterpillar, and when I was a caterpillar there were only two ways to fly – on a leaf's back or in a bird's beak. Neither is particularly appealing. But now I am a butterfly. And, as the song goes, I thank the Lord for 'giving me wings'. I can fly. We are new creatures with new capacities.

### New fuel

Now the Lord doesn't just give us new capacities; he gives us new fuel – his gracious Holy Spirit, working in us. His gracious Spirit wanting to work in us more and more, wanting not only to point us to Jesus, but to make us more like Jesus. Yes, you are who you are, but you are becoming something different, something more like Jesus. That's what we rejoice in. It's the only way most of us could even begin to contemplate talking about modelling godly character, never mind writing about it. After all, if you knew what I was really like, and one or two people do (and they ain't telling cos I have stuff on them and I have friends in low places), if you knew what I was really like . . . I mean the hypocrisy count in this chapter is off the charts. 'Yes,' says my PA, 'but we are all in the same boat.' 'But not,' I say, 'a boat with so many holes in its hull.' But she's right. Yes, I am in no doubt that her boat has fewer holes than mine, but we'd all be sunk without Jesus. We do have a long way to go, but while there may be no room for complacency, there should be room for gratitude for what God is doing in us and what he has already done.

So, as we seek to model godly character, we don't do so in our own strength. We don't grit our teeth and try to summon up some smidgen of love, some atom of patience for that belligerent bad-tempered bully of a centre half in their football team; we go to God. And then maybe one day we suddenly find ourselves behaving in the way we would really like to behave. It's not that we've responded to some moral exhort-ation, really worked hard not to put a neat row of stud marks in his left shin; it's just that we don't react quite the way we used to, and then we catch ourselves thinking, 'Oh, that was unusual. That was good.' And it's not pride or self-satisfaction, it's just a godly rejoicing with God at his work in us. Indeed, it is important to see that Paul does not say that the fruit of the Spirit is doing loving things, doing kind things or gentle things, though no doubt a person who is full of love will. No, the fruit of the Spirit is the living presence of those qualities in us. So, yes, God does do loving things, but he does them because he is love – he just can't help it, any more than an apple tree can prevent itself from producing apples. So God's Spirit forms the quality of love in us, makes us 'love-trees'. God makes us 'patience-trees' so that our responses to situations can somehow not be anything but patient. We can't help it.

And sometimes the quality of the character God has forged in us is so strong that it can overcome the deepest of wounds.

## Ruth's revelation

She couldn't believe it. She really could not believe it. How could he be a Christian? Ruth, after all, had had a tough childhood. She'd gone to a Christian school where she was treated really badly and punished for every little thing. She was taught that she had to go to church on Sunday. And if she didn't, the teachers would punish her and, of course, God would know. And God was a God of anger and fearsome retribution. She left primary school with a huge sense of relief to leave behind the people who had been so cruel and the God who would do nothing but punish her.

Twenty-eight years later she found herself working for Jonathan. They got on well and she counted him as a friend. He was quite simply the best boss she'd ever had. And then it happened. She was talking to a colleague: 'Do you know that Jonathan is a Christian?' So, it turned out, was the colleague.

It just didn't make any sense to Ruth. They were such nice people and she thought so highly of them.

Then, one August, shortly before a week's holiday, Jonathan handed her a letter and an invitation to Alpha. As she put it: 'This resulted in fifteen emails going back and forth between us and me spending weeks on end crying my eyes out about my weaknesses and insecurities. I wanted to accept the invite to Alpha because I didn't for one minute believe Jonathan would invite me to something that wouldn't be good for me, but I was terrified of once more facing a God of wrath and perhaps also more folks to punish and hurt me.'

But she did go to Alpha. And then to a Luis Palau festival, where she gave her life to a God of love and forgiveness and grace, a God she would not have met if Jonathan's loving, kind, godly character had not been so compelling that it overcame all the wounds inflicted on her young heart.

But, of course, Jonathan didn't know anything about Ruth's childhood when she started working for him. Jonathan wasn't 'trying' to be particularly loving; God, by his grace, had made him so.

## Character assassination

Still, even if we can't model godly character in our strength, there is something for us to do – two things. Live by the Spirit, and crucify the sinful nature with its passions and desires (Galatians 5:24). We open ourselves up to respond to the promptings of the Spirit obediently . . . and we seek to become aware of how our sinful nature continues to express itself, and to proactively seek God's help in transforming those behaviours. In Galatians 5:19 21, Paul lists those behaviours: 'sexual immorality, impurity and debauchery; idolatry and witchcraft; hatred, discord, jealousy, fits of rage, selfish ambition, dissensions, factions and envy, drunkenness, orgies, and the like'.

The cumulative impact of such a list, and the extreme nature of some of the behaviours, can perhaps blind us to the ways in which we may be rather more prone to some of them than we might at first suppose. Obviously, if your frontline is a place that you don't go to every day, or even spend much prolonged time in, you may not find yourself having to deal with 'dissensions' or even 'factions', but then again, you might. There are cliques and factions in many a gym and golf club. And dissensions too. And there is a form of 'selfish ambition' in the footballer who commits a 'professional' foul to prevent the opposition scoring, even though they are an unpaid amateur playing for a village kick-about team.

Similarly, impurity on the frontline of a gym or club or school gate does not just manifest itself in predatory promiscuity, whether female or male; it can manifest itself in almost any social interaction. Isn't there a tendency in many of us to pay a bit more attention to the prettier woman or the more attractive man than to others less aesthetically endowed? And don't we swiftly recognize it and resent it when others do it? No, the challenges to character come not only when the pressure is intense; they also come when life is relatively easy. Jesus' words on murder pinpoint the principle: 'You have heard that it was said to the people long ago, "You shall not murder, and anyone who murders will be subject to judgment." But I tell you that anyone who is angry with a brother or sister will be subject to judgment' (Matthew 5:21–22). Both wheat and weeds grow from tiny seeds.

So, we pray for help to walk in step with the Spirit and we put to death the manifestations of our sinful nature through confession and prayer – there is a time for character assassination. When Louise was dealing with the ogre, she no doubt felt some anger towards him that she had to put to death. We have a part in shaping our character.

And so does God. Actually, he's at it non-stop.


## A lesson from the hutch

At that particular time, my frontline, the primary place where I spent my days and tried to make myself useful to other people, was the office of an ad agency just off the Strand. Not that *I* had an office. I had what my colleagues affectionately called 'the hutch' ('a pen or coop for small animals', according to the dictionary). The hutch was a dark, inner space that had been created by the strategic arrangement of partitions and filing cabinets in the middle of a corridor. The hutch was accessed through the gap between a pillar and one of the partitions. The hutch was just big enough for a desk and a chair. The hutch didn't have even a gleam of a glimmer of the mythic glamour of the ad business, but it was *my* hutch, and in my hutch I was as happy as a hobbit.

On that particular day, my client asked me to do a big job and to get it done by the following morning. As I recall, she needed it fast because her boss needed it fast. And I couldn't pass it to a subordinate because I was the subordinate of all subordinates. What the client needed was a complete budget summary across six countries in local currency and in dollars. Now, this was in an age before computers on every desk, before computers on any desk for that matter, before Excel, before terabyte hard drives the size of a fingernail embedded in the cerebral cortices of every executive. This was in an age when an adult might actually be required to do multiplication and long division themselves. Now, as it happened, I was able to do long division. Still, reconciling budgets was not the kind of task I relished at the best of times, never mind when I had so little time to do the reconciling. And so it was that a rancid, resentful reluctance simmered away under whatever shiny veneer of professional enthusiasm I was able to muster.

Still, I worked hard and long and late, got it done and faxed off the summary early the following morning. The last sentence of the covering letter read: 'I am your most obedient and humble servant.'

Later that morning, the Board Director in charge of the business asked me to come into her office. Her office wasn't a hutch. It had a real door. And four walls. And a wide window overlooking Somerset House with a view to the Thames. And she had more than one chair. Her name was Monica Tross. She was wonderful and she taught me a great deal about a lot of things. She said, 'That was a terrific piece of work, Mark . . . thoroughly spoilt by the arrogant way you ended that letter.' She was right, of course. I had allowed my resentment to get the better of me and had managed to turn victory into defeat, to sour a good piece of swift, competent, helpful service with an outburst of petty, petulant, puffed-up arrogance.

But here's the thing: where had the King of the universe decided to teach me about my pride? Where had the King of the universe decided to try to teach me about what good work really looks like? Where had the King of the universe decided to try to teach me about being a servant, a cheerful giver, a worker who works for his glory? Not in the sanctuary of the church – though he does it there too. Not in my home group, nor with my prayer partner, nor over coffee with Christian friends . . . but right there on my frontline, right there in the middle of my ordinary day.

And who was the Lord God, the King of the universe, choosing to teach me all those good lessons? Was it a preacher? Was it a home-group leader or a discipler? No, it was my wise – though not necessarily church-going – boss.

Makes sense, doesn't it? After all, if you were the King of the universe and you wanted to teach, rebuke, correct and train your people (2 Timothy 3:16), would you confine it to Sunday mornings and Wednesday evenings and twenty minutes at the start of every day?

The frontline isn't just a primary context for mission; it's a primary context – though not the only one – for Jesus to teach us how to become more like Jesus. And if, in the past, he's been so intent on getting his message out that he's been prepared to work through a donkey (Numbers 22), how very surprising it would be if he also didn't seek to work through the humans we come in contact with and the situations we face day by day.

## Character and fruitfulness

I wonder if you can see some ways in which you might have been fruitful in character on your frontline. I wonder if there is someone you know whose character you admire, whom you might compliment, who doesn't realize that they are a dolphin. And would be encouraged to know it.

And I wonder what the pressure points are for you on your frontline.

Who are the people, what are the situations where you know you've needed God's Spirit to help you?

What are the situations where you wish you'd called on God to help you? Where you wish you could have been a wee bit different? Where you hope you could be a bit different next time?

Of course, Paul's list of the fruit of the Spirit in Galatians is not meant to be exhaustive. There are other lists – the Beatitudes for a start, and lists in Romans 5:3–5; 1 Corinthians 13:4 7; Philippians 4:8; Colossians 3:12–17; James 3:17; 1 Peter 3:8–9; and 2 Peter 1:5–7. And there is a tremendous emphasis throughout the Bible on humility as opposed to pride, and on selflessness as opposed to selfishness. What's clear from all of this is that character matters, that God is making us into people with particular kinds of qualities. Yes, as we shall see in the next chapters, there are things we are meant to do, concrete actions that spring from our character, but character is important in itself – character is not just displayed through actions, but through our emotional posture. I can do the right things but not in a manner that is notably kind. I can do the right thing under pressure but not in a manner that is joyous or marked by an elemental peace.

Here, joy doesn't mean that we have to be highly carbonated, effervescent people gambolling into every encounter like exuberant puppies. There are plenty of joyous Christian people who aren't extroverts but who have something about them, something luminous, something that makes you pleased to see them walk into a room – even if you never get to talk to them. One of them walked into our home the other day, unexpectedly, a woman who had had such significant challenges in her family life for so many years, a woman who right now has another huge difficulty to face, and yet, and yet, still there was this elemental joy about her, this deep well of shalom – the peace of Christ reigning in her heart. Still.

In Galatians, Paul summarizes it all as freedom. Christ's grace and love frees us from the power of sin and the hamster wheel of legalism, our vain efforts to try, try, try to do the right thing in our own strength. Christ's love graces us with that deep assurance of his love which gives us joy and peace and allows us to be other-centred. As John puts it, 'We love because he [God] first loved us' (1 John 4:19).

As we are given an ever-expanding picture of who God is and what he has done for us, as we recognize more deeply how lavish his mercy is, how patient he is to us, that begins to express itself in both our attitudes and actions. The one shapes the other. Right attitudes lead to godly behaviours, and right behaviours can also begin to shape our attitudes – doing the right thing even with gritted teeth, even when we don't

want to, can indeed enable us to do the right thing next time
with a bit more of a smile.

May the Lord shine through you this very day.

## A prayer for this moment

Father,
thank you that you want me to become
more like your Son.
Grant me that same desire.
Forgive my cherishing of ungodly thoughts,
and my persistence in ungodly actions.
And work in me by your Spirit,
that I might turn from the darkness of my sin
and walk in the light of your grace.
To your glory may it be.
Amen

## Questions for reflection

Can you think of someone who has modelled an aspect of
godly character to you? Might you encourage them by telling
them? Doris - Died

Can you think of ways in which you have modelled godly
character on your frontline? work. w Friends

Which fruit of the Spirit do you feel in particular need of right
now? Gentleness

## Exploring further

Charles H. Dyer, *Character Counts: The Power of Personal Integrity* (Chicago: Moody Publishers, 2010).

Pamela Evans, *Shaping the Heart: Reflections on Spiritual Formation and Fruitfulness* (Abingdon: BRF, 2011).

James Bryan Smith, *The Good and Beautiful Life: Putting on the Character of Christ* (London: Hodder & Stoughton, 2011).

R. Paul Stevens and Alvin Ung, *Taking Your Soul to Work: Overcoming the Nine Deadly Sins of the Workplace* (Grand Rapids: Eerdmans, 2010).

Tom Wright, *Virtue Reborn* (London: SPCK, 2010).

Work doesn't take us away from God;
it continues the work of God.

Eugene Peterson


It is not by great things but by great diligence
in little everyday things
that thou canst show great love for God
and become greatly holy and a saint of God.
Few ever do great things and the few who can do them,
can each do but few . . .
everyone can by the grace of God be faithful
to what he knows.
Your daily round of duty is your daily path
to come nearer unto God.

Edward Pusey

# 5.

## M2: MAKING GOOD WORK

Meredith\* was stuck.

In fact, the whole project was stuck. Not stuck because a contractor hadn't turned up or had gone bust, not stuck on the construction of the sea wall, or the esplanade, or the regeneration of the seafront or the construction of the shops. No, the whole big multi-million-pound regeneration project couldn't be completed because none of the highly competent major contractors Meredith knew could figure out how to stick some granite plaques to the sea wall.

Now the granite plaques weren't just there for decoration; they were there to carry the words that told the history of the town, to make sense of the whole project for townspeople and visitors alike. So the project couldn't be completed until the plaques were up. Like a torch without the batteries, like a car without petrol, like a locked house without a key, like King Richard III without a horse . . . the size of the problem was entirely disproportionate to the scale of the consequences.

*And Meredith, experienced, highly competent, godly, senior project manager that she was, had run out of options.*

*And then it occurred to her. Something radical, a way to approach the problem that she had never tried for something like this, something small, something everyday, something ordinary. Meredith, experienced, highly competent, godly, senior project manager that she was, decided to pray.*

*And after she'd prayed – call it coincidence if you like – an idea popped into her head. Yellow Pages. So she flipped open the tome. And there it was: 'Sign Makers'. 'Sign Makers,' she thought, 'know how to stick things to things.' So she called the number of the sign-making business that she passed most days on her walk to the sandwich shop. 'Oh, yes,' the man said, 'we know how to do that. In fact, we've recently done something similar just fifteen miles down the coast.'*

*And so it came to pass that the granite plaques were fixed to the wall and the project was completed.*

*And something else started.*

*It is no exaggeration to say that Meredith's life has never been the same. Not only on the frontline of her day job. She realized that God, the King of the universe, the Creator of all things, the Redeemer of all, God cared about the little things she did day by day. All of them – at work, at home with her kids and husband, at the shops, in church . . . Now she finds herself praying about pretty much anything. And things happen – too often to call it coincidence. Of course, sometimes things don't happen the way she'd like, but she's taken them to God who is, she knows, working on a rather large regeneration project of his own and has his reasons and his schedule. And doesn't get stuck.*

Work. We all have work to do. Little things, big things. Obviously, if your frontline is a full-time or part-time paid or voluntary job, what you do occupies a big chunk of your time.

But, even on frontlines where you don't actually have a job as such, there are usually things you do. And the way you do them can make a big difference.

Take the gym, for instance: you either wipe the sweat off the handles of the cross trainer or leave it there; you either remove the 50 kg barbells from the bar or leave them there (and if they are 50 kg barbells, it would be very helpful to most of the rest of us if you did remove them); you either leave your towel in a squidgy heap on the changing-room floor or you pop it in the wash bin . . .

On every frontline there are things we do.

Biblically, work isn't what we get paid to do; work is anything we do that isn't just for fun or recreation. Still, if we are honest, most of us don't really believe that most of the things we do day by day are important to God, never mind part of his big purposes in time and eternity.

Does God really care about how we arrange biscuits on a plate, or how we conduct ourselves in the queue at the super-market, or whether we manage to fix granite plaques to a sea wall in southern Scotland? Get real.

Well, all our tasks certainly do matter to God. On that, the Bible is startlingly clear: 'Whatever you do,' Paul writes, 'work at it with all your heart, as working for the Lord, not for human masters, since you know that you will receive an inheritance from the Lord as a reward. It is the Lord Christ you are serving' (Colossians 3:23–24).

Whatever you do. Not some things you do, not 47% of the things you do, not the things you do in the church, but 'whatever you do'. And God would hardly ask us to do whatever we do with all our hearts, if it were not of some significance to him, even if we ourselves may not think it significant at all.

The question is, why is it significant? In this chapter we'll explore that question and then go on to look at the implications for what we do and how we do it. What does 'good work' look like?

## Why work matters to God

Why is our work significant to God?

Let's begin at the beginning with God's own work of creation.

So here's a question: Why doesn't God create Adam on Day One?

Why does God create Adam on Day Six?

Because if God had created Adam on Day One, it would have been dark and there would have been nowhere for him to stand.

God is love, so everything God does is an expression of that love. God doesn't plonk Adam down in the middle of a sweltering, arid desert, or on top of a windswept Himalayan mountain, or on an iceberg floating nonchalantly in the North Atlantic; God puts Adam in the garden of Eden, in a fertile garden of delight, as Eden means in Hebrew. Eden is not only beautiful, but comes complete with clean air to breathe, fresh water to drink, delicious, nutritious food to eat, animals to look after, and God's presence to enjoy in the cool of the evening.

What has God done? God, like a parent preparing a room for their first baby, has created a perfect environment for Adam. God has created a context for human flourishing. And one of the ways Adam and Eve will continue to flourish is by working. God does not tell Adam and Eve to manicure the garden as if it were some treasured heritage show garden to preserve in perpetuity for posterity; he tells them to work it – that is, to release its potential, just as the fictional Crawleys must find ways to release the potential of *Downton Abbey*'s farmland.

Eden was perfect but it was not mature.

There was work to be done. And work is an instrument God uses to get things done that he wants done.

Tragically, Adam and Eve rebel. And everything is marred. Including work. It will no longer be easy: 'By the sweat of your brow you will eat your food' (Genesis 3:19). However, that does not mean that work has lost its original purpose. It is still part of the plan for each of us. It is still one of the instruments God uses to get things done that he wants done – animals cared for, creation looked after, people fed and clothed, people given shelter and education, music created, beauty crafted and good work made available. God is still concerned to create a context for human flourishing. Eden was perfect. And there was work to be done. Our world is far from perfect, and there is work to be done.

Indeed, as we saw earlier, Christ came not only to save souls, but to reconcile 'all things to himself'. And until he comes again to complete the renewal of all things, as he promises in Revelation 21:5, we are called to be involved in making his world as much like he would want it to be. Everything we do should serve this divine purpose. Our work is meant to contribute to creating a context for human flourishing.

Interestingly, the yearning to create a context for human flourishing is in most of us. It's what someone does when making a home, creating a place where they and their friends can come for rest and refreshment. It's what a party host does – tries to create an environment in which everyone is free to celebrate. It's what a good manager does – tries to create a context that brings out the best in the whole team. As one senior manager put it to me, 'My job is to roll the rocks off

Dorey's house of healing.

the runway so other people can fly.' It's what a good team member does too – tries to do their job in such a way that it creates a better context for others to flourish in – punctually, well, graciously. And that's what good church leaders do – try to create an environment in which people can flourish as whole human beings in Christ.

Work is God's instrument to get things done that he wants done, for the benefit of people and to his glory.

So, for example, God wants people fed. But what does it take to feed people in a modern economy? You need farmers to do a good job, to have good seed, good fertilizers, reliable tools and good facilities for storage. You need good distribution systems to get the produce to processing and packaging facilities, good drivers to transport it to good shops, good people to shelve it and sell it, good marketeers to alert people to the benefits of the products, and good cooks to prepare it. In sum, apart from providing the rain and sunshine for the crops, God needs a lot of people to do a lot of work in order to achieve the goal of getting people fed.

Now, as it relates to the frontline of paid workplaces, this command to be involved in doing work that creates human flourishing has very profound implications. As we have seen over the last decade, when bankers lose sight of their God-given mandate to serve society, hundreds of millions of people are dumped into grinding poverty. When National Health employees are not managed with care and concern for their welfare, in the end, patient care suffers. This applies to every sector of employment: Christians have a duty not only to do their work well, but to do all they can to ensure that the work they do benefits others. And that, in many contexts, can present significant challenges. Some products should not be made, some services not offered – however profitable – some programmes not aired, some processes stopped.


## Good work in action

Still, there are all kinds of ways we can make good work. Indeed, when we look at God's work in Eden, we see that he: *THe House*

- Creates order – like a farmer reclaiming some wasteland, or a chambermaid restoring Eden to a trashed hotel room . . .
- Generates provision – like any man or woman who works to provide for themselves and others . . .
- Brings joy – like making a delicious cake, or a splendid new version of the computer game FIFA, or a new version of a tax form that is really rather easy to complete . . .
- Creates beauty – like a flower-arranger, or a decorator, or a child setting the table rather nicely, or an engineer working at Jaguar Land Rover's Coventry plant on the design of the new F-Type . . .

How might the tasks you do bring order, provision, joy and beauty into the world?

You stack shelves with the product name facing forwards so the item is easier to find – thank you; you empty our rubbish bins, rather tidily, so that we don't become the local McDonald's for the neighbourhood foxes – thank you; you change a nappy so your grandchild doesn't suffer nappy rash – ah, that feels better, doesn't it? You make a computer that's easy to use – thank you, thank you, thank you; you craft a guitar that sounds wondrous – thank you, Mr Fender.

## Taking the biscuit

I can't paint, I can't draw and I can't sculpt, but before you pity me my lack of artistic talent, you need to know that I can arrange biscuits. In fact, I love arranging biscuits. I also like eating them, but it gives me an inordinate sense of satisfaction to create pleasing patterns of oblongs, squares, triangles and circles, to contrast colours and textures – hazel-brown, smooth milk chocolate snuggling up to creamy, crumbly shortbread; or shiny orange foil against ebony dark Bournville. Sometimes I fashion a festive wreath of overlapping roundels or a many-spoked wheel. Sometimes, if there are lots of different shapes, I like to lay them out on their china canvas to create all the serene balance of a Mondrian painting.

Yes, I know it's not much more than kindergarten craft. But the thing is, often, very often when I bring in a plate of biscuits and try ever so hard to lay it nonchalantly and unassumingly on the table for our guests, someone says something like, 'Doesn't that look great? It seems a pity to ruin the picture.' Of course, they always do ruin the picture. And they are meant to. Biscuits are made for eating – that is how, as Yoda might say, they fulfil their destiny.

But there's been some fleeting experience of joy that lifts the spirit. Partly it may be amusement that an apparently adult man should go to such lengths in the presentation of a few Bourbons and Hobnobs. Partly, whatever their judgment of the aesthetics, they perhaps feel honoured by the effort made. But it is, I believe, more than that – there's a joy in seeing something usually randomly arranged turned into some satisfying and, dare I say it, even beautiful pattern. There's a joy when something ordinary is done as if it were important. I know it's just biscuits; I know someone who doesn't know Jesus can create beautiful patterns; I know it seems trivial. And then I look at the extraordinary delicate patterns of veins on a single red leaf of the Acer tree in my neighbour's front garden – and God takes my breath away.

Work is how we make ourselves useful to other people. And bring joy and beauty. ( and order )

Work is service. And though we may serve others through it, ultimately, as Colossians 3:24 clarifies, whoever our earthly boss, it is the Lord Christ we are serving.


## Changing rooms, changing lives

Keith is a decorator. He's been self-employed for twenty-five years, changing rooms, changing houses. For the first ten years of his life, he certainly tried to do a good job, but he wouldn't say that he involved God in his work at all. He worked to earn money. Then he was in a car crash. The car flipped over. For Keith, it was a prod from God. From then on, as far as his work was concerned, he had two aims: to earn money and to give money to God. That was it for twelve or thirteen years.

Then, one day after a talk in church, a light bulb went on in his head. He realized that when he's decorating he's helping other people to lead the lives they need to lead. He's helping a woman look after her sick husband because she can't do the decorating. He's helping an older man who can't do the DIY any more. He's helping a family with a disabled child to make a home that really works for them. He's serving God by serving people. He's not really doing anything different in his actual work, but his mindset has totally changed. As he told me, 'I'm not doing it for the money any more. I'm not doing it to give money to the church. I'm doing it for God. That's my service. And it has totally transformed my life.'

We serve God by serving others.

At its best, therefore, work is an expression of love, because almost every task we do has the potential to have either a positive or a negative impact either on people whom God loves or on the cosmos he has called us to work and take care of.

And so it is that when God commands us to do 'whatever we do with all our hearts', it is not just because he wants us to be wholehearted and a positive witness to people around us; it is because making good work is important in his mission of renewing and restoring the universe.

## Working for God

Still, *how* we do our work does matter.

What is the appropriate way to work for the King of the universe?

Hard, energetically, competently, carefully? But isn't that just a recipe for the kind of driven, performance-based, contemporary Western 'workolatry' that is corroding our souls, exhausting our bodies, withering our hearts and blighting our relationships? Are we competing for some Christian Employee of the Month award, not only trying to tick all our boss's boxes, but the great big appraisal form in the sky?

## Working for Dad

Yes, we work hard, but we work for God. And God is not a Pharaonic slave-driver. God is not primarily a boss, though he is the Lord to whom we owe swift and joyous obedience. God is first and foremost our Father, and we are his sons and daughters. So we not only work hard, energetically, competently and carefully; we work with love in our hearts for God and for the people served by our labour. We may or may not love all the tasks we do, but we are called to do all the tasks we do with love for others and out of gratitude for God's overwhelming love for us.

Furthermore, the fact that God is not first and foremost our boss, but first and last our Father, means that we can trust him to give us the resources to do the things we have to do – hour by hour, day by day, year by year. A good boss never leaves his workers without the resources for the task. And God, being our Father, knows there is more to life than work, which is why he commands us also to celebrate a Sabbath rest.

What a difference to know that our Father is with us in our daily tasks. What a difference to know that we can draw on his wisdom, his Spirit, his Word, his people to help us do the things he has called us to do . . . whatever they are.

And we see that personal concern lived out in, for example, Genesis 2:19:

> Now the LORD God had formed out of the ground all the wild animals and all the birds in the sky. He brought them to the man to see what he would name them; and whatever the man called each living creature, that was its name.

God is interested. Notice what it says in the text: 'to see what he would name them'.

God comes down to see what Adam would name that large pachyderm with a nose that doubles as an arm, because he is interested in Adam and he is interested to see how Adam uses his powers of observation and his language skills to name the animals and birds, and distinguish them from one another.

Why is he interested? Think of a parent as their three-year-old presents them with their first squiggly, scrawly drawing. With what intensity they examine it, perhaps simply rejoicing in the effort made or the gift given, or the rudimentary skills emerging. Or perhaps wondering, 'Is this a Picasso I see before me?'

Similarly, God the Father is interested in you. And he is interested in how you use the talents, the freedoms, the opportunities, the power, the resources that he has entrusted to you. Indeed, often it is our ability to do something that opens up a missional opportunity – whether in a workplace frontline where our competency opens the door, or in a leisure-time frontline.

## Game over?

J (his name) had spent around eight years running a Monday night football game, as a way to reach out to the teenagers on the rough urban estate where he lived. It had flourished, but as the core group grew older, got jobs, and a few moved away, it was clear that the activity had run its course. J was, as footballers say, absolutely gutted, not because the game had stopped, but because he now had no easy way to continue to relate to the boys in whom he'd invested so many years of his life. He prayed with disappointment and a certain amount of bewilderment in his heart: surely this can't be the end.

About three months later, Gary,* one of the footballers, called him out of the blue and told him that he was thinking of starting a football club with a number of the lads who used to play on Mondays. He didn't ask J to play, but he did ask J if he'd like to get involved. The club will need a chairman, someone to sort out the paperwork, make sure everything is above board and so on. Now J happens to be a barrister, so he knows how to sort out paperwork and make sure everything is above board. It was the perfect role for him, giving him an excuse, no, a reason, to be as closely involved with the team as he wanted. He couldn't have come up with a better idea himself: in fact, he hadn't come up with any ideas himself; God was at work.

And it was the tasks J could perform that opened the mission door. As well as his character.

Indeed a couple of weeks later, Gary called him and asked him to collect the subscriptions from the players. 'Why can't you do it?' J asked. 'Oh, they don't trust me with the money – they think I'll do a runner or spend it on booze.'

So, if God is interested in what we do and how we do it, how then are we to do our work?

## Good work, godly work?

Ian is a joiner who is a Christian. A while back, he fixed five of our dining room chairs that had become worryingly wobbly, wobbly to the point where one began to fear for one's coccyx.

Ian used his talents, his freedom, his power and his resources in our service, choosing a particular glue that doesn't set too rigidly and provides flexibility – important in caring for a chair. He did good work. He did good. And our coccyxes are safe. And we all sit more comfortably and eat more peacefully as a result.

But Ian could have fixed our five wobbly chairs well, even if he weren't a Christian. And he would still have served us, he would still have done good and we would still have been grateful to him and grateful to the Lord for him.

So, what's the difference between good work and godly work?

Sometimes, not much. At least, not much on the surface.

Christians haven't cornered the market on excellence in any field. As my boss Mark put it, 'Everything Jesus did was consistent with him being God, but not everything he did made people think, ah, that has to be God.' Doing godly work is not primarily about excellence, though God is interested in excellence. And Jesus, we are told, did everything well (Mark 7:37). Godly work is good work, done in a godly way for God.

And the godly way to do work is to do it for his glory and in his strength.

## The work of people and the praising of God

Jesus puts it like this: 'In the same way, let your light shine before others, that they may see your good deeds and glorify your Father in heaven' (Matthew 5:16).

Notice he does not say, 'Let your light shine before others, that they may see "you" and glorify your Father in heaven.' He says, 'Let your light shine before others, that they may see your *deeds* and glorify your Father in heaven.' Our deeds are important. Jesus wants our work to result in people praising his Father.

So our prayer for our work is not only that we might do it well, that it might serve other people, but that God might be praised.

And this radically alters how we might see ordinary everyday tasks.

Praise after all is not just the acknowledgment that Jesus is Lord. Demons know that. No, you cannot praise God unless you have some inkling of who he is and why he is worthy of praise. You can't praise God unless you believe in him as good. So, our daily tasks have a conversionist motive in themselves – that they will cause people to praise God. Our tasks may achieve many things, but they are also a component of God's evangelistic strategy. They are not all of it – people need to hear the good news – but our deeds are part of it. Here's an example.

### Holy carving

About thirty years ago, my parents had dinner with Michael and Rosemary Green. Now Michael was one of the foremost evangelists of the twentieth century. At the time, no-one in my family was a Christian. But, about fifteen years later, after I'd become a Christian, I discovered that my parents had had dinner with one of the foremost evangelists of the twentieth century. I was very excited to find out what they talked about. So I asked my mother: What do you remember about your dinner with one of the foremost evangelists of the twentieth century? Some brilliant answer? Some wonderful insight? Did he bring up the gospel over the pre-prandial sherry or wait until the wine had softened up their defences? What penetrating question paved the way for a masterful presentation of the gospel?

This is what my mother remembered from her dinner with one of the foremost evangelists of the twentieth century: 'He carved the meat with such dignity.'

A few years after this somewhat puzzling response, I went to a lecture by Michael Green. Afterwards, I waited in the queue, eager to ask him a question. Finally, my turn came. 'Michael,' I said, 'fifteen years ago you had dinner with my parents.' 'Yes, yes, how are they?' 'And there's something that I've been meaning to ask you. My mother recalls only one thing.' 'Yes'. 'She remembers how you carved the meat with such dignity.'

Quick as a flash, he said, 'Well, I suppose I would. After all, the animal gave its life for me.'

His biblical understanding of the graciousness of God's provision and of the dignity of creatures that God had given life to was so deep that it came out in the way he carved the meat. And not only that, his distinctive holy way of carving was discernible by someone who didn't yet believe in Jesus, and was remembered by them for over thirty years.

The most mundane action can carry the fragrance of Christ.

Certainly, it's the case that poor work done with a bad attitude is very unlikely to create a good platform for talking about the gospel. Conversely, when you serve others well, when you do your bit, pull for the team, your words about Jesus are more likely to be well received. And even if we haven't seen a holy carver at work, we've all known the difference between work well done and work well done and suffused with love.

We have perhaps been to someone's house for supper and found ourselves being served some splendid repast – smoked Alaskan salmon with fresh dill, a twist of Sicilian lemon, strewn with Beluga caviar and followed by a Japanese Kobe beef steak with fresh-picked Finnish wild forest mushrooms, Jersey new potatoes and honey-glazed Norfolk carrots with toasted Turkish almonds – (I can dream, can't I?), and yet for all the meal's splendour and culinary skill, we have somehow felt less than truly welcome. By contrast, we have perhaps also had the experience of popping round to someone's house, being served beans on toast and scrambled eggs (with or without a lot of freshly milled black pepper) and feeling as if we've been treated like royalty. It's the same in a coffee shop – there are some baristas who are there to sell you a cup of coffee, and others who don't just wish you a nice day but actually want to make it nice. Quality of life is determined by the quality of love.

## In God's strength

Godly work is not only done for God's glory; it is done in God's strength.

It is very easy to go day by day and never ask God's help in the things we do day by day. Of course, if we're under enormous pressure – if we are caring for someone who is long-term sick, if we're tired, late and the supermarket queue is a mile long, if a client is barking at us – then we are quite likely to pray. However, the real challenge is to ask God's help in the things we do quite well already. And most of the things that most of us do day by day by day we probably do quite well actually – whatever our frontline. But Jesus says this: 'I am the vine; you are the branches . . . apart from me you can do nothing' (John 15:5).

What Jesus means here is not entirely obvious. After all, lots of people do lots of things quite well, without knowing or acknowledging Jesus. And lots of those who call on the name of Christ do lots of things without any prayer for his help or any conscious reference to him. So what might Jesus mean? Might he mean that things done in our own strength, in our own will, do not count as fruit as far as he is concerned, however impressive they might be?

The Tower of Babel was an impressive construction project, but it was a job done in direct defiance of God's will. The ark was an impressive construction project, but it was a task done in direct obedience to God's will. Everything we do is meant to have God's logo on it, to be God-honouring. And he doesn't put his logo on tasks with which he has nothing to do.

Beyond that, perhaps God is inviting us into a different kind of adventure in our daily living – not just a call to a different attitude, but to a different set of possibilities.

What might happen if we invite God into our tasks – the ones we find difficult and the ones we find easy. What amazing things might happen if we asked Jesus to come into things we already do quite well actually? Might it be just a smidgen better? Might it be an awful lot better? Might the response of others be much more positive? Might he teach us something? Might he do a miracle?

When God gets involved in our tasks on the frontline, who knows what might happen?

### A prayer for this moment

Father,
grant me this day your wisdom, your strength, your Spirit,
to help me do all I do for you,
that it may be helpful to others,
bring contentment to my heart
and glory to your name.
Amen

### Questions for reflection

What tasks on your frontline do you usually pray about?

What tasks on your frontline might you particularly bring to God?

In what ways have you seen God work through your work?

## Exploring further

Ian Coffey, *Working It Out: God, You and the Work You Do*
(Nottingham: IVP, 2008).

Ken Costa, *God at Work: Living Every Day with Purpose*
(London: Alpha International, 2013).

Mark Greene, *Thank God It's Monday: Ministry in the
Workplace*, 3rd edn (Bletchley: Scripture Union, 2001).

Timothy Keller with Katherine Leary Alsdorf, *Every Good
Endeavour: Connecting Your Work to God's Plan for the World*
(London: Hodder & Stoughton, 2012).

Tom Nelson, *Work Matters: Connecting Sunday Worship to
Monday Work* (Wheaton, IL: Crossway, 2011).

We love because he [God] first loved us.

1 John 4:19

# 6.

## M3: MINISTERING GRACE AND LOVE

*I used to be part of a wonderful community of Christians close to Watford. It was a church, it was Baptist and it was in a town called Bushey. Rather unimaginatively, but not surprisingly, it was called Bushey Baptist Church. And there was a man there called Peter. At the time I was working at the London School of Theology, but Peter knew that I was more than a little interested in what was going on out in the everyday working world. So every now and then on a Sunday he'd come up to me and pass on a few newspaper articles about work, business or culture that he thought I might find interesting.*

*Is cutting out helpful newspaper articles ministry? Or is it just a nice thing to do?*

*Now I had immense respect for Peter and loved his company, but I hadn't known him for that long and I wasn't in his home group and I don't think I'd ever done anything in particular for him. But there he was, thinking of me as he read his newspaper on his daily commute, holding my interests close enough to his consciousness to*

*spot an article that might interest me. And apart from that, it took*
*him time and effort. He had to pull out the articles and keep them*
*somewhere and remember to bring them to church, and he had to*
*give up some of his fellowship time after church to pass them on.*
*And he had a big job and two teenage daughters and significant*
*responsibilities in the church. He didn't **have** to do it.*

  *Grace is like that.*

Grace doesn't have to. But grace does. Grace is on the lookout
for opportunities.

  Love doesn't have to. But love does. Love is alert to
possibilities.

  The Shunammite wife of 2 Kings 4 doesn't have to proactively extend hospitality to the itinerant Elisha, and she
certainly doesn't have to encourage her husband to build and
furnish a room on their roof so Elisha can have a place to stay
'whenever' he passes by. But she does.

  Jesus doesn't have to heal Simon Peter's mother-in-law
(Matthew 8:14–15). No-one asked him. He doesn't have to go
over and heal the paralysed man who couldn't scramble into
the pool fast enough – the man didn't even cry out to him
(John 5). Jesus doesn't have to set out for the centurion's
house just because the elders of a synagogue think he should
(Luke 7). He doesn't have to turn water into wine (John 2).
He doesn't have to raise Lazarus from the dead (John 11),
doesn't have to come to earth, doesn't have to die on a cross.
And the resurrected King of the universe certainly doesn't
have to do anything as mundane as make hot, grilled fish on
a lakeside fire as his fishermen disciples haul in their boats
after a long night's work (John 21).

  Jesus doesn't *have* to do any of those things, except in so far
as love and grace and obedience to the Father's will compel
him. Grace doesn't have to. Love doesn't have to. But they do.

## Beyond 'have to' . . .

In the last chapter we explored how we can do the things we usually have to do in a godly way. But grace and love are more than 'have-tos', so in this chapter we will focus on how grace and love might express themselves by taking initiatives or simply by responding with greater generosity. There is, after all, a joyous generosity, a lavishness, about God's grace. God the King of the universe doesn't have to forgive us our outrageous rebellions, he doesn't have to send his Son to die for us, he doesn't have to send his Spirit to comfort, counsel, change us. He doesn't have to lavish on us 'the incomparable riches of his grace' (Ephesians 2:7). Indeed, such is his grace, his personal care, that it expresses itself not only in big things but in little things. Indeed, perhaps sometimes when we think of 'ministry', we set the bar far too high. It's as if it has to be some evangelistic initiative or some major project – looking after the homeless, working with teenagers, counselling someone or staying up all Saturday night to help clubbers out of the gutter . . . praise God for all of that. But at root, ministry just means serving others.

Ministry is love in action: taking a moment to engage with the checkout person, noticing the 'invisible' people, saying thank you to the caretaker of your kid's school or the cleaner in the changing room at the gym, or getting up early once in a while to say 'thank you' to the people who empty your bins, calling a carer and just asking if there's anything you can pick up from the shops when you go . . .

Remember the story Jesus tells in Matthew 25:

> Then the righteous will answer him, 'Lord, when did we see you hungry and feed you, or thirsty and give you something to drink?' . . . The King will reply, 'Truly I tell you, whatever

you did for one of the least of these brothers and sisters of
mine, you did for me.'
(verses 37–40)

Jesus sets the bar pretty low. Actually, Jesus probably sets the
bar a lot lower than any of us would: a cup of water. That's
it. Yes, Jesus is talking primarily about serving people who
follow him – his brothers and sisters – but the principle still
applies: we minister love and grace through small acts done
unselfconsciously to serve others. And often our left hands
really don't know what our right hands have been up to.

Perhaps you've had the experience of someone coming up
to you and telling you about something you said years ago
that was so helpful. Or telling you about a card you wrote to
them when they were going through a hard time that made
all the difference, and that they still have. And actually, you
have no memory of it at all. You honestly think they've got
the wrong person. When did I ever do that? You didn't have
to. You just did it. And God worked through it.

You don't have to volunteer for the social committee in
the student hall, you don't have to become the parent rep
for your child's class, you don't have to join the committee of
your neighbourhood association . . .

I wonder what ministering love and grace looks like on
your frontline.

What might it look like in a workplace, for example?

## Counter-culture

There's a reason why the public reception counter at your
average county court is behind reinforced glass screens and can
only be accessed through locked doors. Actually, there are a

number of reasons: solicitors are often impatient and rude to staff to the point of disdain, and customers usually arrive stressed, often upset, and occasionally volcanic. In such circumstances, it's pretty easy to start seeing customers as a nuisance, irritants, the enemy. Indeed, staffing the public reception counter instilled an entirely understandable measure of fear in pretty much every member of the team. Except Chrissie – all of 5 ft 5, 110 lb and not-even-a-brown-belt-martial-arts-badge-to-her-name Chrissie. Chrissie rather enjoyed it, though she was careful to keep such psychological bizarreness to herself.

One day, a young man called Dave* came to the counter, asking for help to fill in a form for an *ex-parte* non-molestation order, which is an emergency court order to prevent somebody from hassling you. As such, it is a pretty important form to get done quickly and get done right. It soon became apparent to Chrissie that Dave had a mild learning disability, since every question had to be explained several times. A long queue was forming at the counter, a long queue of usually stressed, possibly already upset and potentially angry people. And Chrissie realized that significant time would be required to help Dave in a situation that made no allowances for such a lengthy focus on one person. The choice was to tell Dave that she couldn't spend any more time with him or . . . Chrissie went to her section manager and asked if a colleague could staff her counter while she helped Dave. When the form was complete, Dave expressed concern that he wouldn't be able to get to his day centre in time for lunch. He could phone them but he needed help to do so.

Now it is not in the job description of a county court clerk to help customers make phone calls, but Chrissie came out from behind the locked glass partition and walked Dave to the public phone in the entrance hall, called the number for him and explained the situation. 'Yes, of course,' the day centre carer said, 'we'll put some food to one side for him.'

When Chrissie sauntered back behind the safety of the glass walls, her colleagues thought that she was mad to go to so much trouble for a bloke like Dave, a nuisance really. But, as Chrissie put it, 'I saw a person whom God loved, a person who was valuable in my Father's eyes, someone in trouble who needed just a little help. And it really didn't seem like such a big deal.' Not to Chrissie, but it was a big deal to her colleagues and to Dave, precisely because it wasn't a deal at all – grace doesn't do deals.

Take another frontline. What might ministering love and grace look like as you go to the supermarket?

### Topshopping or superqueuing?

Yes, there's the opportunity to chat to the checkout staff, but, if the supermarket were your frontline, you'd go to the super-market with a whole different mindset, a whole different attitude to time. You wouldn't be trying to get out of there as fast as possible. You'd be paying attention to people, not time.

You might pause and smile at the mum with three frantic-ally 'tired' children. You might ask the person behind you in the queue if they are in a hurry and want to go in front of you. You might even just join whichever checkout queue is closest to you, without scanning the length of each queue, swiftly calculating not only the number of trolleys in each queue but how many items are in each trolley, and not only the number of trolleys and items but the age, gender and, therefore, the likely packing and paying speed (PPS) of the various shoppers (avoiding the old, the infirm, the woman with three children, the middle-aged men, and any queue with someone who's already genially chatting to someone and is therefore likely, heaven forfend, to waste precious seconds doing the same with the cashier). And you'd not only be calculating the number of trolleys, the number of items and the shoppers' likely PPSs; you'd be factoring in an assessment of the cashier's competency and alertness, based on your prior experience of their performance, the current angle of their shoulders and the level of brightness of their eyes.

No, if the supermarket were your frontline, you wouldn't be doing any of that – you wouldn't have read *Queuing for Dummies* or enrolled for an MA in Advanced Queuing in Postmodern Britain. No, if the supermarket were your frontline, you wouldn't be doing any of those things; you'd pray as you made your way there, asking God to give you a nudge if there's anyone in particular he wants you to talk to, you'd allow a bit of extra time for those chance encounters with people you know and people you don't, you'd get to know the staff, you'd get to know the manager . . .

Of course, ministering grace and love on your frontline isn't just about doing 'little' things. Sometimes we know very well that we are going out of our way. It's not exactly convenient for Nehemiah to leave the plush comfort of the imperial palace and his relatively easy job, to go and rebuild the far-off, crumbling city of Jerusalem in the face of intense opposition. Ministry isn't always convenient. It's not exactly an attractive proposition for Ananias to go and welcome the Christian-killing Saul as his brother, and pray that he would receive his sight. Ministry isn't always convenient.

This is perhaps why Jesus highlights visiting the sick and those in prison (Matthew 25:36–44). Even in the ancient world, it would never have been convenient. In the case of visiting someone in prison, there was the high risk of contracting shame by association – Paul, for example, specifically commends Onesiphorus for not being ashamed of Paul's chains (2 Timothy 1:16). In the case of visiting the sick, there was the significant risk of contracting the disease yourself. Even today, for lots of us, visiting a sick person almost always means not doing something that is already in our schedule or in our mind to do, and there's often awkwardness, particularly if the illness affects the person's mind. So we do need to consciously ask for God's grace, his empowering presence to help us keep going or even just to help us get started. We don't always minister out of strength or even out of an abundance of resources – whether money or talent or time.

The good and generous Samaritan had coins in his purse to pay the innkeeper to care for the mugged stranger (Luke 10:35), and he generously gave them. We, however, don't always have the resources ourselves, though we do know a God of unlimited resource who may have some gift he wants to give. And may prompt us to participate in its delivery.

In Acts 3, Luke tells us about a man crippled from birth who was carried to the temple gate every day to beg. Now the apostles Peter and John must have passed him day after day as they went up to the temple. Indeed, they must have passed many other beggars too. On one particular day, though, something different happens. We are not told why this day is different from every other day. We are not told why they stop to talk to this particular beggar, but it seems more than likely that they were prompted to do so by God. Now, the beggar was asking for money, but Peter and John had no silver and gold to offer. But they had been given some intimation by God that they might offer something to the disabled man that he wasn't even asking for, perhaps didn't even conceive was possible – his complete healing. And so they command healing in the name of Jesus (Acts 3:1–8).

Of course, God continues to do miracles, but whether or not we see God working in such an immediate and obviously supernatural way, ultimately we do not minister grace and love out of our own resources, but in partnership with an omnipotent Lord. Some situations are beyond us. But not beyond God.

What, I wonder, is possible when God is with us?

## Text for today

One of Frank's* frontlines was the pub, not because he was a drinker of anything much stronger than a Coke, but because it was just the place he felt he was meant to go to from time to time. He'd been chatting to a friend, and after the friend left, he sensed that God wanted him to go and talk to a particular woman. Now many a young man has had that sense in the past, but this woman was certainly fifteen years older than Frank and was accompanied by two men, one of whom had his arm in a sling. Frank was keen to obey, but just hadn't got a clue as to how to go about beginning a conversation, so he said to the Lord, 'You've got to give me something, some way into a conversation.' Nothing came, but he continued to pray and extraordinarily, for the first and so far only time, decided to pull out his phone and randomly type in a text to himself with his eyes closed. When he opened his eyes, this is what he saw: 'Toes☺'. You have got to love that smiley face.

Now the woman in question was wearing boots, so if there was an issue with her toes, it certainly wasn't visible. With some trepidation, he walked up to the trio and said to the woman, 'Sorry to intrude, but I am a Christian – don't worry I am not going to preach at you, but I felt that God may have said that there may be something wrong with your toes. Does that mean anything to you?' The woman looked somewhat amazed and took off her right boot and showed Frank her foot. The bottom half of her foot was completely white as a result of a circulatory problem. It turned out that it had been like that for four months and self-evidently the things her doctor had tried hadn't worked.

'Well,' said Frank, 'if God has told me about this, he probably wants me to pray for healing. Would you mind?' 'No,' she said, 'I'm an atheist, but go ahead.' Frank prayed. And before four pairs of amazed eyes, the foot healed. And then Frank prayed for the arm that was in a sling, and the man suddenly had a much greater freedom of movement. A good conversation followed.

Great is the Lord.


## Generous forgiving, generous living

Ministering grace and love on the frontline also means practising forgiveness.

Forgiving your boss for breaking her promise, for blaming you for something you didn't do; forgiving that teacher for their sheer incompetence; forgiving the checkout person for messing up the transaction and having to call over the manager to get it done . . . Frontlines have people on them. People who may not be feeling that well or who are over-whelmed, people who make mistakes, people who sin. It's not just us. Forgiveness liberates. And so does seeking forgiveness. When we blow it, we need to seek forgiveness, not only for our own sake, but to give other people the opportunity to be liberated from whatever bitterness or anger they might be harbouring towards us. Forgiveness heals in two directions.

At root, whether convenient or not, ministering grace and love is at root about generosity. Generous living. It's about taking the focus off ourselves and proactively thinking about how we might help someone else. It's about being alert to opportunities to serve someone, being on the lookout at the school gate for the new parent who looks lost, or the colleague who is clearly not doing that well, or the person who's been absent for a while, or noticing the little boy in Costa who's bored with the only game on his mum's phone and is now a little fractious as she and her friend chatter away, and offering his mum your phone so he can play Temple Run 2.

Generosity, however, leads us beyond merely meeting a lack or a need. Grace and love go beyond the acceptable minimum or the way things are usually done – the homeless person is not just given a meal, but a really great meal. Indeed, there is more to ministering grace and love than kindness. Love is about wanting and seeking the best for someone else. And that can be expressed in a variety of ways.

It could involve taking the risk of helping a difficult person see that they are being difficult. It could involve telling the golf club captain that a member is unwell and might appreciate a call. It could involve praising a colleague who is your rival in front of the team because actually they did do a good job. It could involve finding a way to help someone you work with realize that there is a job out there somewhere that would suit them much better. It could involve starting a business to create jobs for people who don't have them.

Of course, sometimes you start small and you find yourself involved in something much bigger.

## Patient care and gospel outcomes . . .

David's frontline was his office, and for some time he'd been disappointed by the lack of any real opportunities to talk about Jesus directly. He'd prayed, he'd asked advice, but nothing seemed to happen. And he knew that it wasn't the kind of place where you could just launch in. That, he was convinced, would be counter-productive. But he prayed, he sought advice from Martien, a pastor friend who told me this story, he studied all the ways Jesus ministered, he made himself accountable to Martien and he tried to stay alert to opportunities. Anyway, one Monday, one of his colleagues, James, failed to turn up to work.

No-one thought much about it – probably just a spectacular weekend – but when he didn't turn up the following day, David called him, even though he wasn't a particular friend of his.

'Are you OK?'

'No, I'm feeling terrible. I haven't been able to get out of bed for three days.'

'Is anyone looking after you?'

'No, I live alone and my family are miles away.'

'Have you got the right medicine?'

'I haven't even got any food.'

Anyway, to cut a long conversation short, David went round to see James that evening, got him into the shower, changed his linen, took him to the doctor, got the medicine, bought food and went to see him every evening for a week. During that week, James never asked David a single question about why he was doing all he was doing for him.

However, within a week of James's return to work, David found himself inundated with opportunities to talk about the gospel. James had told everyone what David had done. And he found himself accosted in the lifts, in the corridors, in the cafeteria; his colleagues simply couldn't understand why he'd done it. As Martien put it, 'David replied carefully and humbly to all who asked, "It is nothing I did; I have chosen to model my life on the life and teachings of Jesus and I think what I did is the kind of thing he would have done. I don't do it very well, but I do my best."'

Of course, that is a pretty spectacular example, but the essence is grace and love. David didn't have to look after James, did he?

So, as you think about the people on your frontline, I suspect that there have been times you've given them the equivalent of a glass of water . . . and not really thought much about it. But I wonder, as you pray for them, whether the Lord will show you some way you might extend grace and love to them.

I began this chapter with a story about Peter, a man in my church who cut out newspaper articles to help me in the work God had given me to do. It was very encouraging. And I wonder whether you can find ways to support other Christians in your church or in your home group on their frontlines, to help one another be more fruitful there. Yes, in prayer, but perhaps in some practical way too. When her husband's team were going through a really tough patch, so tough that many of them were hardly getting home at all, Rachel and her daughter baked a big batch of her exceedingly brilliant brownies for them and sent them to the office in the post. They didn't have to, but it had a huge impact – like a Red Cross parcel to a POW.

Grace doesn't have to. Love doesn't have to. But they find a way.

Grace to you this week.

Grace through you this week.

## A prayer for this moment

Lord, help me to see
these people,
this place,
and these issues
with your eyes and your love.
Lord, help me to bring
to these issues,
to this place,
and to these people,
your wisdom and your love.
Amen

## Questions for reflection

Has anyone ever done something for you that they didn't have to do? What impact did that have on you?

Thinking about your frontline, what things might you do that you don't have to do but might be a blessing?

## Exploring further

Wendy Billington, *Growing a Caring Church: Practical Guidelines for Pastoral Care* (Abingdon: BRF, 2010).

Michael Mitton, *A Heart to Listen: Learning to Become a Listening Person* (Abingdon: BRF, 2010).

David Moore, *Who Is My Neighbor? Being a Good Samaritan in a Connected World* (Colorado Springs: NavPress, 2010).

Bill Peel and Walt Larimore, *Workplace Grace: Becoming a Spiritual Influence at Work* (Grand Rapids: Zondervan, 2010).

Michael Wakely, *Generosity: Big-Heartedness as a Way of Life* (Leicester: IVP, 2004).

Culture is the way we do things round here.

Derek Worlock, former Archbishop of Liverpool

# 7.

**M4:** MOULDING CULTURE

*I come from a Jewish background. You can tell just by looking at me, and if you can't, then I suggest you make an appointment with your optician. Now there are a lot of things I love about Jewish culture and indeed about the particular kind of Jewish culture I grew up in. There were, for example, the family rituals – Friday night candles and the family always together, big gatherings at Passover, getting presents from grandparents at Chanukkah and, splendidly, at Christmas too – any excuse – a battalion of great-uncles and aunts always so very warmly enthusiastic to see you . . . And there was also a curious variation on a common custom – bringing gifts when you visit people.*

*Any time anyone came round to our house, whether for a festival, or supper, or just a cup of tea, they'd bring a gift: a box of chocolates, a vase, something . . . And even today my brother can't even pop round my house for half an hour without bringing something. He's over fifty now, but the parental question is still booming in his head: 'What are you taking?' Often my mum or dad would protest as a gift was proffered, 'Oh, you shouldn't have . . .' And the giver would say what sounded like 'For handling'. The phrase puzzled me for years. It's actually a Yiddish word from the German for 'trade': Handlung.*

*'For Handlung' meant that the gift was given so you could use it as a gift to take to someone else's house. Indeed, sometimes the giver would actually say, 'For handling' as they gave it to you, as if they had absolutely no expectation that you would use it yourself, but would simply pop it in a cupboard until the day you needed something to take to someone's house . . . who in turn might pass it on. Indeed, on at least one occasion, I am completely convinced that we were given a box of chocolates that we had seen before. In fact, it was so old that the colours were fading on the packaging.*

*Now behind that innocent custom lay a whole set of values – honouring a host, not taking without giving, giving another person the freedom to do what they wanted to do with a gift, not wasting things – we'll never eat those chocolates, particularly now they're four years old, but someone else might – the value of modesty and self-deprecation – it's no big deal, it's nothing special, give it away . . . though of course, sometimes the gift was special, lavish even . . .*

*'For Handlung' was part of our family culture . . . the way we did things.*

And that's Archbishop Derek Worlock's definition: 'Culture is the way we do things round here.' Every family has a culture, every community, every workplace, every team, every church, every home group, every frontline – a way of doing things round here. Some of it good, some of it not so good, some of it downright destructive.

In the culture of Jesus' time there were ways of doing things that he affirmed: going up to Jerusalem for the pilgrim festivals. There were things he criticized: Pharisees making long salutations in the marketplaces and hogging the best seats in the synagogue. And there were things that were neutral in the sense that in themselves it didn't really matter if they were done one way or another. So, for example, in Jesus' culture, teachers usually sat down to teach; in ours we usually stand up. But, as long as the learners can see and hear, it doesn't really make any difference.

Indeed, the more we understand the culture of Jesus' time, the more surprising and revolutionary are some of the things he chose to do. So, when Martha complains that Mary is not helping to prepare the meals, but sitting listening to Jesus teaching, his response is not just to affirm her choice of education over hospitality, but to clarify to Mary, Martha and his male disciples that, in a patriarchal culture in which adult women did not sit at the feet of rabbis to be discipled, it was wonderful for Mary to do that. Similarly, in a culture that valued male testimony in social, religious and legal contexts above female testimony, how counter-cultural it was for Jesus to choose to communicate the reality of his resurrection to women first. Men and women are equal in Christ's eyes. His way of doing things expressed his values, just as my family's *Handlung* expressed their set of values.

Our values and beliefs shape our behaviour.

Take a culinary example. I love eggs, particularly scrambled eggs, soft but not runny, with lots of freshly milled black pepper and salt. However, for most of the last two decades, scientific research seemed to indicate that eggs contributed to high levels of cholesterol. So I ate fewer eggs. The teaching I had received, the doctrine I had accepted, the beliefs I held about eggs led to a dramatic reduction in my egg consumption.

But then about two years ago a new era dawned. Scientific research revealed that eggs could be consumed in reasonable numbers without affecting cholesterol levels. The doctrine on eggs had changed, and I was liberated to live life to the full.

My eggcup runneth over.

Indeed, now all that remains for my joy to be complete is for someone to discover that eating large quantities of Stilton is actually the key to longevity, fitness and octogenarian mental acuity.

Beliefs and values shape action – whether we are aware of it or not.

One family's values impel them to buy a Prius rather than a Lamborghini, or not to have a car at all. One school's values lead them to put a very high premium on academic attainment above all else, rejoicing in A*s but not really paying any attention to character, growth of self-confidence or social skills.

## Divine values in diverse cultures

In the Bible, we find God's people living in a whole host of different cultures that are shaped by very different values – Abraham among pagan tribes, Joseph in Pharaoh-centric Egypt, Daniel under the capricious, totalitarian dictatorship of Nebuchadnezzar and then under the legally constrained reign of Darius, Esther in the degenerate, inwardly oriented court of Artaxerxes, Jesus in Roman-occupied Israel, Paul in intellectual Athens and idolatrous, superstitious, occult-ridden Ephesus . . . and so on. In all those contexts, and in all ours, God's people are called to allow God's values, God's Word, to shape their character and their behaviour.

We see this, for example, as God seeks to prepare the exodus generation to create a distinctive culture in the Promised Land. The laws and stipulations he provides in Exodus, Leviticus, Numbers and Deuteronomy are there to guide the people's thinking and action in every area of life – from sacrifice to

sexual relationships, from farming to festivals, from commerce
to caring for the poor. However, two central values shape all
the rest, as Jesus makes clear when he is asked: 'Teacher, which
is the greatest commandment in the Law?' His answer:

> 'Love the Lord your God with all your heart and with all your
> soul and with all your mind.' This is the first and greatest
> commandment. And the second is like it: 'Love your neighbour
> as yourself.' All the Law and the Prophets hang on these two
> commandments.
>
> (Matthew 22:37–40)

In other words, the primary shapers of any culture should
be first a total commitment to loving God. And second, a
total commitment to loving people created in God's image –
a commitment, therefore, to seeking their best, seeking their
blessing and flourishing. In that regard, the primary tests of
any culture – national, organizational or familial – are: does
this culture honour God, and does it seek God's best, God's
shalom for all its people? A family ruled by a bullying parent
fails the test. An organization run for the benefit of its bosses,
and not its employees and customers and fellow citizens, fails
the test. A nation interested only in the prosperity of its own
people fails the test.

Not surprisingly, since God is love, this same rule of love
applies in the New Testament. God is love, and he commands
his people to live in his ways of love as his Spirit forms the
loving character of his selfless Son in them. And so it is with
us, whether we are Scots or Scousers, Cockneys or Celts, we
are commanded to create ways of doing things that help
people flourish. Indeed, ultimately, our ways of doing things
in our cultures are either positive or negative. They either help
people flourish as whole human beings or they make it more

difficult – eat five a day or smoke twenty a day; tell the customer everything they might need to know or only tell them what they ask about; have a national day of rest every week so it's easy to meet friends and family, or have Sunday trading and live with the reality that several of my extended family and friends have to work and we can't get together so easily.

So, as disciples of the Creator-Redeemer Son, who believe that he has commanded us to cooperate with him in creating contexts for human flourishing, how can we, as it says in Jeremiah 29:7, not only pray for but also *seek* the shalom, the peace and prosperity of the frontline God has called us to? Well, we might begin by praying for an ability to see what is good or not good in the way things are done on our frontline and then seek ways to affirm or change them.

What's good about the way people do things on your frontline? What's worth cheering? And what isn't good? Not only for others, but for us? In Romans 12:2, Paul exhorts the Christians: 'Do not conform to the pattern of this world, but be transformed by the renewing of your mind.' Paul knows it's pretty easy to end up behaving like everyone around you – gossiping because everyone does; being a bit too concerned about the sculpting of your biceps because everyone else is; being cynical about customers/bosses/lecturers/students/ teachers/pupils because everyone else is . . . So we look for ways not only to change our own behaviour, not only to show love to individuals, but to seek to create systems that are 'loving', to change the way things are done around us for the good and the good of all. And, encouragingly, you can begin to change the whole dynamics of a culture through quite small things.

Take, for example, a primary school in an urban regeneration area. Lots of the kids are on free school dinners. Many of them have never experienced what it feels like to sit down for a family meal. Now their canteen is a little drab and rather noisy, and the kids zing in and out like Formula One cars refuelling in the pits. It's the way things are done. But Rachel, the assistant head, wanted to teach them that meals are special, for conversation, not just for food, and she wanted to make them feel special. So the school bought tablecloths for all the tables. The change has been remarkable. The table-cloths absorb some of the clatter of crockery and therefore make the atmosphere calmer, more conducive to chatting. But more significantly, the presence of tablecloths instantly communicated that eating together is special and that kids are too. In the end, the tablecloths enhanced the quality of relationships, the quality of love, between pupils, and between pupils and teachers. Small things can make a big difference.

## The power of food

Diane's* team at work was fine, but she had been wondering how she could bring them together a bit more, develop a greater sense of camaraderie, just oil the wheels. So one day she invited her team into her office for a short break with coffee and, perhaps inspired by Marie Antoinette, for cake, a cake which, as it happened, she'd baked herself. It was just a cake, but her team were bowled over that she should make such a lovely personal gesture for them. And the team loved the opportunity to relax together. Pretty soon other people in the team volunteered to bake something. And it became a weekly feature.

Later they branched out into sharing 'nostalgia sweets': flying saucers with the transparent tops that you stick your fingers through, sherbet fountains with those liquorice tubes that you are theoretically meant to suck the sherbet through but which inevitably clog up, so you get to do what you really wanted to do all along – just glug it back.

Now what was happening here was not just that the calorie count was rising; what was happening was that memories were being shared, relationships deepened, and levels of understanding and trust were rising like the sponge in a jam roly-poly.

'Where did you get that recipe?'

'Oh, I got it from my great-great-grandmother who came over from Moldova in 1892.'

'Oh really. So did mine.'

And so on.

Of course, our employers don't pay us to eat cake and chat about Rooney or recipes or long-lost relatives. However, recent business research (e.g. *Harvard Business Review*, April 2012) does reveal that organizations where there are regular informal opportunities for people just to talk to one another are more productive *and* more profitable. Good relationships are good for business.

So what had Diane done?

1. She had identified an aspect of the culture that could be improved.
2. She looked for a kingdom solution.
3. She tried it out, putting in time, investing money and making herself a bit vulnerable – the cake might not have turned out to be so good and people might not have got on.

But the cake was great, and the team was working in a way that was much more like the way Jesus would have wanted them to. And interestingly, Diane didn't have to do it all herself. Other people who didn't know Jesus were all involved, all contributing, all giving of themselves to others, all tasting that his ways are good.

Now, the initiative she took was actually quite small, but it carried a concentrated dose of kingdom values – generosity, kindness, selfless service, proactive reaching out to others. It was a Trojan mouse which opened the gates to a different kind of behaviour, a mustard seed of hospitality that grew into a tree that others came to shelter under.

> The kingdom of heaven is like a mustard seed, which a man took and planted in his field. Though it is the smallest of all seeds, yet when it grows, it is the largest of garden plants and becomes a tree, so that the birds come and perch in its branches.
>
> (Matthew 13:31–32)

Diane put the interests of her co-workers and indeed the interests of the company to the fore and sought to create a context in which all might benefit. She had focused on enhancing the quality of the relationships in the team, on creating a context in which they would feel loved and could learn to love one another better. 'Love thy neighbour' in action. But impelled by her desire to express her love for God on her frontline.

And you can do that in almost any context.

Take your neighbourhood supermarket.

One older woman decided that her frontline was her local Costcutter. So she set out to develop relationships with the staff. She's not their chaplain, just a customer, but now when she goes into the shop, two of the staff tend to give her a hug. It's not the way things are usually done in contemporary supermarkets, is it? It's not that there was anything necessarily bad about the way that shop was operating, but could she enhance it?

Take a street. If that's your frontline.

A street perhaps where nobody really seems to know anyone, where people are happy to share a cup of sugar, or keep a lookout when you're on holiday, but not really a street where people know one another. What might it take to change a street culture like that?

Maybe you begin by deliberately walking up and down it at times when people are about, just to get to know a few people, passing the time of day, noticing who's on their own, offering to mind a child for a couple of hours, and when someone moves in not only going over with a macaroni cheese and saying 'Hi', but inviting them to come and meet a few of their other neighbours who you may not know yet either – a good excuse to knock on their doors. Or perhaps it's a couple of you getting together to call on people, just to say that you are praying for people in the street, and if they have anything they'd like prayer for now or in the future, just let us know . . . and leaving a card . . . Or maybe it's getting together to throw a street party or . . .

## Estate planning

Andy and Kate had been working through a DVD (*Life on the Frontline*) with their home group and had begun to ponder the question: 'Where is our frontline and how can we have an impact there?'

As it happened, they were about to move into a new home on a new estate, so there wasn't a lot of time for prolonged reflection, what with lawyers, mortgages, utility companies, sorting through what to take, what to give away, what to throw away, reminiscing fondly over some souvenir, or trying to remember what on earth possessed them to have ever even contemplated buying that vase in the first place, never mind keeping it in the loft for the last decade – just in case . . . And in the midst of all that, they realized that their frontline was to be their new estate and that they might try to create a different kind of community. Too often, they felt, neighbours, especially on new estates, never really got to know one another. They didn't want their neighbourhood to be like that. And because, in God's providence, they were part of the first batch of six families to move in, they were perfectly placed to set the tone.

So, soon after moving in, they popped little cards through the doors of the other five houses, introducing themselves and suggesting that everybody got together at their place for a drink that coming Friday – less than a week after moving in. Now, most of us like to make a good impression when we invite people round to our houses for the first time. We prefer the curtains to be up, the carpets down, the boxes away, the pictures straight and that ghastly vase safely hidden in the loft . . . but, as Andy said, 'People don't come round to see your Laura Ashley lightshade, but to see you.'

Andy and Kate weren't really sure what kind of response they would get to the invitation but, much to their amazement, within half an hour, each household had either popped round, phoned or texted to say, 'What a great idea' and 'Love to come'. This gave them confidence that they had done the right thing and that God was involved.

That Friday, everyone came round for drinks, including another couple who had moved in just the day before. They were all at the same stage – putting up curtains, assembling furniture, trying to find that screwdriver, the plasters, the dog . . . so they all had plenty to talk about.

That evening, doors opened – literally and figuratively. And Andy and Kate have been able to serve their neighbours practically: cutting grass, assembling furniture, as well as just taking a break over cups of tea or an evening drink. Impressively, when someone offers help, people are actually able to accept it, even though they are British. In fact, they quickly became comfortable enough with one another to ask for it. In sum, the sense of communal commitment is spreading: people are spending much more time engaging casually than you'd expect outside the constant camaraderie of a TV soap like *EastEnders* or *Brookside*, and one neighbour has joined Andy and Kate to help organize a street barbecue and plan an event to integrate the next batch of neighbours.

It's early days, but Andy and Kate are convinced that the positive relationships they have will make gospel conversations more likely to occur and more natural when they do. Still, they know that, even if none of their neighbours ever becomes a Christian, they have helped make their community a better place to live.

**Culture at work**

And what if your frontline is a workplace?

You look to introduce or reinforce something that carries the kingdom DNA you believe is needed.

Maybe you work for a company that seems totally driven by profit, profit, profit, so you suggest they have a tombola at the Christmas party in aid of refugees. Or you propose a special award for contribution to corporate morale. You fly a flag for a different set of values. Or even for the values that are in the company publicity. After all, you can tell a culture by its heroes, by what it honours and what it rewards. One high-tech, US-based media company I worked with had annual awards in their European HQ not only for Most Valuable Player, but for Eternal Flame, Unsung Hero, International Awareness and Rookie of the Year. Those awards reflected their commitment to a set of values.

- Most Valuable Player: a commitment to excellence
- Eternal Flame: valuing long-term loyalty
- Unsung Hero: valuing high-quality work in low-profile jobs
- International Awareness: valuing the importance of cultural sensitivity
- Rookie of the Year: encouraging new talent

It's the same in any context – home, school, club, and indeed church. The people we honour and the stories we choose to tell in a Sunday service reveal what's most important to us. So, one of the ways we can begin to change a culture is to change the stories we choose to tell, and to broaden the range of people we choose to honour publicly.

So, to participate with God in creating a more kingdom like culture, consider these questions:

What's the culture of your frontline?
What are the values that shape it?
Who are the heroes?
What stories are told?
What do you dislike?
What do you like?
What might make it more kingdom-like?

Of course, we may not be able to change the whole culture of our book group, or our football club or our workplace by next

Friday, but we might be able to change the culture of our team or our bit of the team. Indeed, precisely because culture is expressed in a whole host of little, as well as big, things, culture can also begin to be changed by a range of little things:

- The way we affirm and honour others around us
- The letter we write in appreciation of a faithful friend – in a digital world the physical speaks potently
- The Christmas card we send that includes something we've appreciated about a shopkeeper, a colleague, a plumber
- Choosing to apologize in a culture where no-one takes responsibility
- The decision to ensure no-one has anything against us
- The offer to spearhead the club's recycling initiative
- The 'quote for the day' that you stick on the end of your email

Of course, we also need to address the way things are done and how the organization is structured and managed. Sometimes a big issue rears its head. And one 'M' leads to another. Here's a story about a big change. It's longer than some of the other stories because big change often takes longer.

### *January 2011*
New year, new appraisal system: could be helpful, could be wearisome, could be liberating, could be destructive. This one, as far as Grant* is concerned, is likely to be as beneficial as playing pass the parcel blindfold with a live grenade – everyone is going to suffer and someone is going to get badly hurt. In the new system, 15% of employees have to be ranked 'below standard'. And if you are ranked 'below standard', you lose your bonus and most of your inflation-linked pay rise.

Grant is a senior project manager in a multinational manu-
facturing company, and he has three issues with this new
system.

It arbitrarily changes the terms of everyone's performance
evaluation. Up to this point, you could be the least talented
member of a team and still be performing well above standard
– a mere Gareth Bale in a team full of Ronaldos. This, after
all, is a blue-chip company making outstanding products for
a discerning global market. It's one thing for a company to
seek to improve the quality and performance of its people;
it's another arbitrarily to call their work 'below standard'. It
is unjust.

Secondly, Grant feels it will corrode relationships and team
morale, since it is likely to set up unhealthy rivalries within
previously harmonious teams: people's focus will no longer
be on doing the best they can for the team, but on doing the
best they can to ensure that they are not in the bottom 15%
– and that someone else is.

Grant's third problem with the system is a practical one:
no-one in Grant's team is actually performing below standard.
If he complies with this process, it requires him to lie and
to be involved in unjustly punishing a valued member of
his team.

However, HR systems that are rolled out from the mountain
tops of multinational companies are, like the laws of the Medes
and Persians in Daniel's time, rarely amenable to change.

Someone is going to be hurt.

Grant prays, Grant ponders and Grant seeks advice. He
returns to work and makes his views known to those above
him. He speaks up for truth and justice. He knock, knock,
knocks on heaven's door in prayer but the system is not for
turning. And so, he assigns Richard* to the 'below-standard'
box. No bonus. A below-inflation pay rise.

And we could leave the story there.

Grant has discerned injustice, prayed, sought advice, made a stand on someone else's behalf, and he's taken a risk by challenging the laws of the Medes and Persians. He's done what he could. He's been faithful and fruitful. Praise God for all of that.

And sometimes that's where things end – in injustice.

And sometimes one injustice can lead to another.

## *May 2011*

Grant's senior manager has acquired an over-negative opinion of Richard. Grant fears for the employee's future, particularly because this senior manager has a particularly forceful and intimidating communication style. So he prays and he consults his wife. She comments, 'If your boss communicates forcefully, then, when the time comes, you too will need to communicate forcefully.' Which, if you knew quietly spoken Grant, is like asking a breeze to behave like a typhoon. Certainly, a whisper can be as effective as a roar, but it's harder to hear a whisper when someone else is roaring. But Grant wasn't just trying to salve his conscience; he was trying to win justice. As Jeremiah 5:28 reminds us, it's one thing to plead the case of the fatherless; it's quite another to plead it to win.

So Grant prays. And he prays to the point where God says, 'I've heard you on this one. Enough already. Leave it to me.'

Time passes, and then on a particular day, the forceful manager explodes at some work done by Richard. Before he knows it, Grant finds himself exclaiming loudly, 'You're out of order. You've gone too far this time.'

He can hardly believe what he's done.

And he waits for the typhoon.

But his boss draws up a chair, sits down and quietly asks, 'Do you think so?' And they talk about it.

Grant reminds me of Nehemiah. Nehemiah was really exercised about something that was not right in the world – the devastation of Jerusalem.

Nehemiah prayed about it, over a number of days.

Nehemiah didn't have the power to change it himself, but he had a boss with power. And a God with more.

Nehemiah prepared himself for an opportunity, and when the time came, Nehemiah, like Grant, acted boldly and unusually. In Nehemiah's case, he allowed the emperor to see that his face was sad, something that those who served the emperor were forbidden to do. And because Artaxerxes respected him and cared about him, he noticed and enquired, 'Why does your face look so sad when you are not ill? This can be nothing but sadness of heart' (Nehemiah 2:2).

And he and Nehemiah had a conversation. The rest, as they say, is history.

Well, we could leave Grant's story there with his bold defence of his team member: Grant's been prayerful, Grant's been faithful and Grant's taken initiative. He's taken a justice-driven, selfless, prayer-drenched, community-supported, bold risk for the sake of another person. Praise God for all of that. But that was not the end of the story.

*November 2011*

The company decides to change the language and terms of their ranking system: the percentage of people ranked in the bottom box would be 10% not 15%, the language used would be 'below peers' not 'below standard', and those so rated would receive half their bonus, as opposed to none, and would get half the inflation-linked pay rise.

'The kingdom of heaven,' Jesus said, 'is like yeast that a woman took and mixed into about thirty kilograms of flour until it worked all through the dough' (Matthew 13:33).

Grant had done a lot of mixing. And so clearly had God. And the yeast had begun to work its way through the whole evaluation system of a multinational corporation.

Maybe it is possible to change the law of the Medes and Persians. More specifically, the change in language reflects a change in philosophy. 'I can accept that I am not as good as others in my team. I can accept that, though I have made a contribution to the business, I may not deserve as much as others, but I still deserve something, don't I? And I do not deserve to be punished with a below-inflation rise if I have done a good job.'

The ethos has shifted – one godly manager has influenced the entire performance appraisal system of a multinational plc. It's not where Grant would like it to be, but it has changed significantly for the better. God told Grant to leave it to him . . . and something remarkable has happened.

Grant accepted his calling and called on his God.

And God spoke. And Grant heard him. And God acted. And Grant saw it.

And we could leave the story there and just reflect on the truth that God is the same yesterday, today and tomorrow, that he answers prayer, that he can find ways round unjust human laws and unjust human practices, that he not only tells *us* to be faithful in the little things, but that he too is faithful in the little things.

We could leave the story there.

But life is sometimes not that simple. The HR department comes back to Grant and asks him to increase the percentage of people in the below-peer box, and Richard will be the one to fill it. Enraged and saddened, Grant tells his boss, the very boss who had had such a negative view of Richard. And Grant's boss tells Grant that he has already informed HR that no such thing will happen.

Grant's boss has become Richard's champion. As Proverbs 21:1 says,

> In the LORD's hand the king's heart is a stream of water
>    that he channels towards all who please him.

And we could leave it there.

### Spring 2012

Richard comes to recognize that the role he was in has changed, and that it no longer truly suits his skills and personal preferences. He therefore approaches Grant to request his support in obtaining a transfer to another function in the business – one with a Richard-shaped hole in the team.

Richard applies for such a position, is interviewed and is now flourishing.

And we could leave it there.

But I don't suppose that Grant or God will.

It is vital to pray and plan purposefully about the frontline we usually find ourselves in and to believe that big things can change, accepting that some things do take time, and that it is good to recognize and praise God for the good fruit along the way, not just for the final outcome.

In most of the examples, the prayer and actions of Christians didn't just benefit one person, but benefited many – all the kids in the primary school, Diane's team, every employee in that multinational. That's what happens when a culture becomes more like a kingdom culture: many are blessed. And sometimes people are not just blessed by a decision to change a culture; the change enables people who are not Christians to discover what it feels like to act in the ways of Jesus.

Here's an example from a teenager.

## Following suit

It's Saturday and it's Open Day at a boys' comprehensive –
Watford Grammar School for Boys, to be precise. One of the
boys arrives, hoping to slip his car into the school car park, but
he's told that, on Open Days, it's reserved for prospective
parents. He gets upset and, after parking in a space far, far away,
he starts telling prospective parents not to send their sons to
the school – it's a single-sex school, your sons will be emotion-
ally impaired for the rest of their lives, incapable of relating
healthily to women. Lots of the boys are furious – they are
proud of their school and have worked hard to show it off
to visitors. The head boy, Matt, has to restrain the prefect in
charge of anti-bullying from taking the law, and the boy, into
his own hands. Some teachers intervene. At the end of the day,
Matt – a Christian – goes home, angry like everyone else.

The next day, as Matt goes for a run, he realizes that the
school community might well give the rebel an extremely cold
shoulder. What should he do? In the event, he 'Facebooks' his
deputies to come to an 8 am meeting the following day.

The head boy tells his deputies his concerns. Naturally, they
should leave punishment of the boy to the teachers, but this
boy runs the risk of being ostracized for the rest of his school
career. It's their job as leaders to build community and
harmony. So they call a meeting of the other prefects and tell
them to make sure this rebel doesn't get bullied, doesn't get
picked on . . . And so they do and, as they do, they taste an
alternative way of doing things; as they do, they taste the ways
of Jesus.

There are perhaps some things to learn from this teenager
about having an impact on culture.

Matt knows why he is there: he is God's ambassador and
he has a clear vision of his role on his frontline; he is there to

help build a relationally healthy, cohesive community. Clarity of mission leads to appropriate action.

Matt understands the culture of his frontline and is therefore able to anticipate how some of the boys might respond.

Matt does not accept that it has to be that way. He does not allow himself to be conformed to the culture (Romans 12:1–2), to the way things are usually done round there.

Matt acts in the interests of others. He is concerned for the welfare of the troublemaker, seeking to limit the damage done to him in the short and medium term. He seeks to bring reconciliation, to bring unity, to be a peacemaker.

Matt's capacity to do the better thing is , however, dependent on his character. Matt, after all, has good reason to be angry. The rebel has soured one of the most important events of the school year, an event that he and his team had worked really hard to make a success. Nevertheless, Matt finds a way to love his enemy. And to do that he has first to disempower the anger in his own heart, to quell any thoughts of revenge, or of taking justice into his own hands.

On the cross, Jesus demonstrates love for his enemies, for those who rejected him, mocked him, tortured him and are killing him. On the cross, Jesus defeats sin. He disempowers sin. He overcomes evil with good. Mission is meant to be cross-shaped, and our capacity to mould culture will in some measure depend on the godliness of our character. Vengeful bosses can't build enthusiastic teams. Judgmental whingers can't create happy families. Inveterate gossipers can't cultivate great school morale.

The character we model has a significant impact on the culture we are able to mould.

Matt, however, doesn't just disempower the anger in his own heart and behave in a selfless way himself; he proactively invites others to behave in kingdom ways. He offers others an alternative way to respond, he offers others a way to do good, to seek the welfare of the community. And, as the other prefects do so, they experience God's wise and good ways for themselves. And perhaps recognize that his ways are good.

Of course, this doesn't mean that those prefects all subsequently applied Jesus' principles of forgiveness to every or any situation they found themselves in. On its own this incident may have had little long-term impact, but it wasn't the only demonstration of God's ways that they had seen or indeed that the Sovereign King of the universe will draw their attention to in the coming years. Our role is to faithfully 'seek and pray for the shalom' of the context he's given us and trust that he will bring good out of it in his time.

### A prayer for this moment

Father,
may my frontline become a place of joy and
justice and shalom.
Give me ears to hear how I might pray,
eyes to see what you would have me do,
and wisdom to do it in your ways.
For your glory may it be.
Amen

## Questions for reflection

What do you particularly like or dislike about the culture of your frontline?

What initiative, however small, might you take to make it better? Ask God to show you.

## Exploring further

Graham Cray, *Disciples and Citizens: A Vision for Distinctive Living* (Nottingham: IVP, 2007).

Andy Crouch, *Culture Making: Recovering Our Creative Calling* (Downers Grove: IVP, 2008).

David A. Livermore, *Cultural Intelligence: Improving Your CQ to Engage Our Multicultural World* (Grand Rapids: Baker Academic, 2009).

Gabe Lyons, *The Next Christians: Seven Ways You Can Live the Gospel and Restore the World* (New York: Multnomah, 2012).

Tullian Tchividjian, *Unfashionable: Making a Difference in the World by Being Different* (Colorado Springs: Multnomah, 2009).

In matters of style, swim with the current;
in matters of principle, stand like a rock.

Thomas Jefferson

# 8.

## M5: BEING A MOUTHPIECE FOR TRUTH & JUSTICE

About twenty years ago, a woman walked into a toyshop in a small Buckinghamshire town called Amersham and talked to the owner about his window display. It was October and the window was full of Halloween paraphernalia. She suggested to the owner, Gary, that he should not be selling such material. She was a Christian and explained why. And told him that God would honour him if he stopped. The owner demurred and didn't change his shop window. Later that year, however, he took all the leftover stock that he would normally have kept for the following year – hundreds of pounds worth – and burned it. He has never sold Halloween paraphernalia since.

At the time it felt like a one-off decision, but the principles behind that decision were to set the future pattern for his decision-making about his business. Today that business, The Entertainer, has expanded from one store in Amersham to becoming the largest independent retailer of toys in the UK, even though they don't open on a Sunday. Of course, Gary knows that obedience to God does not mean that God has to bless his business – there are plenty of godly, *competent Christians whose businesses have failed. At the same time, God is his Father, and Gary is in no doubt that the reason his business has consistently outperformed the overall toy industry is down to God.*

*But how did it all begin?*

*One woman walked into a local shop and spoke up for truth and justice.*

*And even if Gary had ignored her, that would still have been a glorious thing to have done.*

Being a mouthpiece for truth and justice. It's a portentous-sounding phrase and perhaps conjures up images of Emily Pankhurst or Martin Luther King, Jr or Gandhi or sit-ins outside embassies, or a lone, slim figure standing in front of a tank in Tiananmen Square. Still, falsehood and injustice manifest themselves in all kinds of places – in school corridors as well as parliamentary ones, in sitting rooms as well as boardrooms. But we'll come to that later.

I happen to love Britain – and not just for all the obvious reasons: beans on toast, Gary Lineker on TV, Morris dancers without inhibition and the Rolling Stones without end. No, I really do love Britain – for our sense of proportion, our appreciation of eccentrics, our sense of humour, our freedoms. But ours is a corrupt and degenerating society which has lost its moral centre. You can see that in a myriad ways, and in particular in the steady erosion of righteous discernment evident in so many of our major institutions: the parliamentary expenses scandal; the decline of appropriate editorial control at the BBC; criminal practice at the *News of the World*; woeful patient care in a small number of NHS units; the hubris of a small but all-too-influential number of people in the banking and financial services sector; and, though it may seem trivial, the vaunting by one of our leading cricketers of a 'winning-is-everything, don't-walk-even-if-you-know you-are-out' mentality. 'It's just not cricket' used to be a phrase that appealed to the highest standards of personal integrity and sportsmanship. Now, I suspect, no-one would have a use for it, since, if you can get away with it, anything is cricket.

Now, if all that seems rather far away from your own front-line, then the reality is that the cultural forces that blinded so many individuals to the significance of their actions in those national arenas are also busy at work among us all – wherever we are: in the volcanic invective often spewed out at referees by molten, vein-bulging parents on the touchline at kids' football games; in our blithe acceptance of the plumber's nonchalant offer to do the job for cash that makes it hard for a more honest plumber to make a living at all; in the widespread falsification of CVs; and all the casual little lies of convenience that litter our conversations – 'Mum's out right now', 'I'll pop it in tomorrow', 'I don't think I got that email . . .' In such a society, if we are to fulfil our calling as agents of trans-formation, there are things to be done and things to be said.

God hates lies.

> Woe to the city of blood,
>     full of lies,
> full of plunder,
>     never without victims!
> (Nahum 3:1)

And God loves truth:

> LORD, who may dwell in your sacred tent?
>     Who may live on your holy mountain?
> The one whose way of life is blameless,
>     who does what is righteous,

> who speaks the truth from their heart;
> whose tongue utters no slander,
>> who does no wrong to a neighbour,
>> and casts no slur on others.
>
> (Psalm 15:1–3)

God hates the exploitation of the poor:

> For three sins of Israel,
>> even for four, I will not relent.
> They sell the innocent for silver,
>> and the needy for a pair of sandals.
> They trample on the heads of the poor
>> as on the dust of the ground
>> and deny justice to the oppressed.
>
> (Amos 2:6–7)

And he loves generosity and justice:

> But let justice roll on like a river,
>> righteousness like a never-failing stream!
>
> (Amos 5:24)

How then might we be mouthpieces for truth and justice on our frontlines?

It's a risky business telling the truth.

About that, the Bible is uncomfortably clear. Just look at what happens to so many of the prophets. Elijah may triumph in the end, but he spends more than three years in hiding (1 Kings 18:1); Micaiah son of Imlah tells Ahab the truth and ends up in prison on a diet of bread and water (1 Kings 22:1–28); Jeremiah says what God tells him to say and ends up socially ostracized, mocked, beaten and half-dead at the bottom of a well (Jeremiah 37 – 38); Stephen tells the truth and is stoned to death (Acts 6 – 7). Of course, those are extreme cases, but the reality is that an extraordinarily high percentage of workplace whistle-blowers end up not working for the very organization they were trying to protect. On a more personal level, I suspect we all know people who don't like to be told the truth about a situation or indeed about themselves. We may be like that ourselves, but, hey, I won't say anything to you, if you don't say anything to me.

Being a mouthpiece for truth and justice might involve alerting the police to the presence of a gang of drug dealers operating down your street, in which case having some people to pray for you, as Daniel had Hananiah, Mishael and Azariah pray for him, might be a good idea (Daniel 2:17). Speaking up for truth and justice might involve sticking up for your neighbour in a dispute with the local council, or for an elderly parent or an autistic child. It might involve blowing the whistle on an incompetent doctor in your hospital, or on a builder who has fraudulently and dangerously not constructed a building to the required safety standard. It might involve challenging a work colleague about the hours being charged to a particular client, or taking on an unjust appraisal system, as we saw Grant do in the last chapter, or challenging your company to make sure their outsourced cleaners are paid a living wage, not just the minimum wage. Such situations require courage and tact to resolve well. And so do the abuses of power that occur in more common everyday situations.


## One knight in the seminar

Matt was a student, sitting in a politics seminar of around twelve people. One of the students began to speak. The tutor cut her off abruptly and then spoke for a while. Later in the seminar, the tutor forcefully rebuked the student in front of everyone else for not being properly prepared for the seminar. But he hadn't actually given her the chance to deliver the presentation she had prepared. She was visibly upset. Afterwards, Matt said that he would have a word with the tutor. And then he started thinking, 'Should I really be doing this? This is a slightly scary man. He is forceful in conversation and exceedingly eloquent.' It felt risky. Challenging power usually does. But, there again, Matt had promised. And a knight in shining armour coming to the rescue of a damsel in distress, even a trembling knight in shining armour, even a trembling knight without any armour coming to the rescue of a twenty-first-century, highly educated damsel in distress, must be true to his word and engage 'the dragon'. Sir Matt promptly went back and tactfully did so. The tutor, to his credit, acknowledged he was wrong, promised to write a letter of apology to the student and then did so. And the damsel? Well, being a twenty-first-century damsel, and therefore unbound by the patriarchal conventions of her foremothers, well, she got down on one knee and asked Sir Matt to marry her . . . just kidding.

Still, speaking up for truth and justice isn't just about such big challenges.

What do we do when there's a succulent morsel of gossip whisking its titillating way round our sports club, or when someone in the family is being blamed for something they didn't do and they don't know how to stick up for themselves? 'It wasn't like that, Dad. She didn't mean it that way.' Or what do we do when the wrong person is taking the blame at work, or when the wrong person is getting the credit?

So, for example, a parent is whinging on at the school gate about a teacher who she feels is incompetent and lazy, but you're puzzled. You've never heard anything negative from your daughter, only how everyone likes her and appreciates the way the homework gets marked swiftly. Now in such a situation it can still be quite hard to say anything. Brits kind of like to complain. We enjoy seeing other people working themselves into a bit of a lather of (self-) righteous indignation and we tend to assume that the complainer is probably right to some extent. And all that makes it harder to go against the flow.

Now, in that school gate situation we might say something like, 'Wow, that doesn't sound like her at all. I've found her really approachable. I'm sure she'd be mortified if she thought that you had those concerns. Why don't you go and talk to her?' Of course, those words are easier to type than come up with at 8.15 in the morning when you are surrounded by a gaggle of fulminating parents. Nevertheless, finding ways to gently offer a different perspective is a good skill to acquire. And can on occasion be the difference between life and death, as the prophet Nathan might have testified.

### Nathan's nous

You'll recall in the book of Samuel that King David enlists his servants' help to arrange an adulterous assignation with Bathsheba, who becomes pregnant (2 Samuel 11). David then goes to considerable lengths to cover his tracks, but fails and then callously arranges for the murder of Bathsheba's loyal officer husband Uriah. So, when God tells the prophet Nathan to confront David, wisdom is required. David, after all, has already had one man murdered. What's to stop him killing Nathan too?

Now, there might have been a lot of ways for Nathan to try to liberate David from his unconfessed sin. Nathan could have gone straight in and addressed him as a husband: 'What would you do if someone seduced one of your wives?' He could have addressed him in his role as commander-in-chief: 'If you sleep with your soldiers' wives, then pretty soon no-one will fight for you.' He could have appealed to family honour: 'Is this any way for a son of Jesse, of the Bethlehem Jesses, to behave?' Or he might have tried to be more subtle: 'I was having my quiet time today and I found myself reading the Ten Commandments . . . and was once again struck by how liberating they are, particularly the sixth and seventh commandments . . . Thou shalt not murder, Thou shalt not commit adultery . . . Anyway, I just thought I'd share that with you . . . not sure why.'

In the end, Nathan appeals to David in his role as judge, asking him to rule in a case of theft which, on the surface, has nothing to do with adultery, but is similar in its portrayal of the callous, wilful, entirely unprovoked exploitation of a poor man by a rich one (2 Samuel 12).

Still, in this, it's important to see that, when God sends Nathan to confront David, God isn't doing it to condemn David; he's doing it to liberate him from his guilt, to communicate the consequences of what he has done and to restore their relationship. Indeed, when Nathan speaks up, it opens up a better future for David. The truth sets David free. So, when we speak up for truth and justice, our goal is not to win the argument or beat the other person; our goal is the well-being of others to the glory of God. Indeed, the concept of justice in the Bible is not just about impartial legal judgments; it is about right living and fair dealings. Speaking and working for justice embraces a commitment to seek to support all that is righteous and to oppose all that is not – for the sake of others, to the glory of God.

## Bottle and Spirit

Tom* works for a drinks company – not a soft drinks company, but a hard drinks company. He's a Christian, and convinced that God called him into the job. One day, Tom finds himself on a business trip in the Far East. One of the ways that business is done in the Far East is to go out drinking together at the end of the day. Tom has rules about this. He goes with the team and he doesn't get drunk. Now, in the Far East, the kinds of places executives go drinking almost always feature beautiful hostesses. Some are there to serve drinks, and some offer rather more. Tom has rules about the kinds of places he goes to. And he sticks to them.

One evening, his team is out with some suppliers, and Tom realizes that one of his colleagues has taken a shine to a particularly luminous hostess. As the evening proceeds, Tom grows more and more concerned that his colleague, a married man, will proposition her. But what can he do? The place is buzzing, there are suppliers and colleagues and the hostesses . . . but his heart aches and he fervently prays, 'Lord'.

A little later, Tom finds himself in the 'facilities'. By coincidence, perhaps, his colleague is the only other person there. So, as they are facilitating, Tom turns to him and says, 'Are you having a good evening? I can see you have some decisions ahead of you. As your friend, I would encourage you to make sure that the decisions you make tonight are the same as those you'd make tomorrow.'

Now, that is some sentence. And although Tom is a bright, articulate man, he's in no doubt that it came from the Holy Spirit (Mark 13:11).

After about ten minutes, the colleague left the club with the hostess. Tom's heart ached more. A little later, Tom left the club and went back to his hotel room and got down on his knees by his bed and prayed and prayed. A couple of days later, it became clear that his colleague had in fact propositioned the woman . . .

However, she had told Tom's colleague that she wasn't that kind of hostess, and asked if he'd be interested in a long-term relationship. They then stayed up until 3 am just talking, much of it about her sorrow because her boyfriend had left her.

Now there's a thing. The man who wanted to use this woman as a prostitute becomes her confidant. And maybe he learned more about how wrong his impulse to sleep with her was by having propositioned her than if he had simply left the bar at 11.30 pm. He learned that a hostess in a bar can have a life beyond that bar, that a hostess in a bar could be a woman with a heart that's tender, a heart that can be broken, a woman with hopes and dreams for her own life . . .

But what about Tom?

Now there's someone who loves his colleague / neighbour as a whole human being. And is confident that God's ways are good for other people, and cares enough to speak up and make the case for right living. It happened to have been in a bar in the Far East, but it could have been in a McDonald's in the North-West or a living room in the Midlands or an office in Coleraine.

There's someone who believes in prayer, who knows how to call out to God in the maelstrom, just as Jehoshaphat did in the middle of the battle (1 Kings 22:31–33), when there is nothing he can do himself. There's someone who also knows how to pray in the quiet place. There's someone who asked others to pray for that trip before he went, someone who has involved the people of God in a frontline of mission that they themselves will probably never be in. There's someone who is confident in God to act – even if he can't think how.

Bottle, Spirit, prayer and the support of God's people – it's a mighty potent cocktail.

And we do need other people's prayers because sometimes the cost of speaking up can be high.

## Public servant

A while back, I went to a debate at Edinburgh University between Ann Furedi, the head of the British Pregnancy Advisory Service, and Professor John Wyatt, a committed Christian, and, at the time, Professor of Neonatal Paediatrics at University College London. The debate was on abortion, a contentious issue at the best of times, and one that can easily turn sulphuric in the cauldron of public debate. But I came away amazed by the respect, warmth and good humour with which the two disagreed with each other so profoundly. Later, I discovered that they had debated each other before and that Ann had on occasion actually asked to debate with John, not because she usually won, but precisely because she and he both felt that they had the opportunity to make their best case with integrity and respect. John told me this:

> One of the things I learned from John Stott was that it is often more important how you debate than whether you win the argument – we're to model dialogue and double listening (listening humbly and reverently to God's Word and listening humbly and attentively to the world). The other thing I remember him saying is that it's important to engage with the best arguments of our opponents and not their worst. So, rather than creating a straw man and then destroying it – which is what so-called public debate is so often about – there should be a genuine quest for dialogue and understanding.

And he said that, despite the fact that, after giving evidence at a Parliamentary Select Committee, he was publicly accused by a senior parliamentarian of deliberately misreading the results of his scientific research in order to bolster his theological arguments. It was an accusation that was reported in the national press. And an accusation that might have tarnished his international reputation and invalidated a lifetime's ground-breaking and careful medical research on behalf of the unborn and the newly born. It caused John great pain over many months. It can be very costly to put your head above the parapet – wherever the parapet is. And sometimes God doesn't just ask his people to put their head above the parapet on a particular occasion; sometimes he asks them to stand on top of the parapet for years.

## What price the property of integrity?

Jeremy* had just been made redundant after ten years of excellent work for a leading property company that had a wonderful reputation for high ethical standards. His boss, not a Christian, had also been made redundant, but had identified a job for Jeremy in another company that he felt would really suit him. Jeremy told him that he didn't think it was right for him. His boss, somewhat surprised and a mite miffed, asked, 'Why not?' 'Well, I don't think it's the job God has for me right now.' There was, of course, not much arguing with that.

Curiously, the job that Jeremy felt *was* right for him was with a company that had a distinctly dubious reputation. His Christian friends questioned the wisdom of that – it seemed to be a recipe for disaster. Jeremy pursued the opportunity, but he wanted to make sure that the company really knew the kind of person they were getting, so that if ethical issues did arise they wouldn't be surprised by his response. So he not only made it clear that he was a Christian on his CV, but when it came to the interview with the owner said to him: 'You know that I am a Christian and that I try to uphold high ethical, moral and legal standards.' Interestingly, the owner didn't feel it necessary to comment, unaware, as it later turned out, of his company's reputation. But Jeremy, having made his position clear, could join the company with a clear conscience.

Of course, Jeremy knew that people and organizations don't change overnight, that good intentions don't always lead to good actions, but he was convinced that this was the place that God wanted him, even if he might well have to resign on a point of principle at some point.

The first point of principle arose on his very first day. As far as Jeremy was concerned, the action the company wanted to take was not only immoral and unethical, but illegal. The discussions began. People told him that he wouldn't be able to budge the owner on this one. But in the end the owner did budge. On that issue.

Eighteen months later, the challenges are still there. A couple of weeks ago, he was walking his nine-year-old daughter to school. She asked him why he seemed a bit less happy these days. He told her that he had a number of issues at work where people wanted to do something that he felt would be wrong. And that, as a follower of Jesus, he couldn't be part of that, and so he might have to resign. 'Well,' she said, 'that would be the right thing to do. It's a bit like with Ella at school. Some of my friends want me to ignore her, but it's not fair and I won't do it. And they aren't being very nice to me at all.'

I wonder where she learned such integrity.

God clearly sent Jeremy to that company to bless it, but there has been a cost to him and to his family. There is suffering involved and perhaps more to come. It is often so. Evil is not easily dethroned. And our opposition is not always merely flesh and blood. There is a war on (Ephesians 6:12).

Jeremy's challenge was systemic, daily and for the medium term, but for most of us the challenges and opportunities to be a champion for truth and justice just pop up as we are going about our daily lives.

## Training the trainer

Claire was a secretary in a large company. At a time management workshop, the trainer's response to one particular problem was: 'You could just lie – say he's out of the office.' Claire's retort was just as simple and direct: 'Well, no, I couldn't, because I don't lie.' Afterwards she reflected on 'How dreadful that sounded, how pious, how goody-two-shoes.' But on the other hand, why let a highly paid trainer think that their considered professional 'wisdom' is useful when it isn't? Why pretend that it might be right to do something you wouldn't do? Why let someone think that you are a certain type of person when you aren't? And besides, Claire, though quite young, worked for the head of a division, and other staff looked to her as an example. Why let other people think that lying is the right way to handle issues in our division?

If Claire had her time again, she might have said it differently, less forcefully, but there again we don't always get to say it perfectly. And we certainly don't have to say it like other people might. We discover our own ways that suit our personality. In my case, I find a swift right hook particularly effective.

Still, we don't always have the right words, do we? We become tongue-tied, and the other person may just be so much sharper than us. There was one person I was never able to win an argument against or usually even get my point across to. I always ended up feeling stupid and embarrassed and misunderstood and weak and pathetic and cowardly. Afterwards, I'd think about all the clever things I should have said that would have carried the day. Afterwards. But sometimes our job isn't to win; our job is just to run the flag of truth up the flagpole.

Sometimes, speaking up involves us in helping someone see their situation differently.

June* is a midwife doing another day's work in the maternity unit. Another day of blood, sweat, screams, tears, words that people don't usually use in front of strangers . . . and in the end joy. And Stacy* comes in. On her own. No husband and no mother. It's unusual. They get to talking, as you do over the hours, and June probes a bit and hears that daughter and mother have not seen each other for seven years, hears the daughter announce that her mother will never see her grandchild.

And in the course of the conversation, June finds the right moment to say and the right way to say, 'You've got it all wrong. It's not that your mother has a right to see her grandchild; it's that your daughter has a right to see her grandmother.'

Seven days later, Stacy turned up on her mother's doorstep with the baby.

June completely changed the lives of three generations of a family. She spoke up, and it opened up a new and better future for a whole family. God's person in God's place in God's timing. For June, looking after mother and child meant more than helping to ensure a healthy delivery; it meant giving the child a relationally healthy family. June didn't have to *say* anything about a true and good way to be family. That's not in a midwife's job description – but it is in a Christian's. The truth sets people free. Christ sets people free.

So we stick up for truth *and* we stick up for justice – righteous ways of living as well as righteous law, fair dealings as well as fair legal judgment.

## Justice for others

Claire, the secretary we met a few paragraphs back, had noticed something. A team in her department had just completed a big project, and everyone involved was given a bonus. Everyone except two people. Two people who had worked with the team for months, but joined a few weeks too late to qualify. Technically, no-one had done anything wrong – the bonus terms were clear and had been properly executed. Still, Claire didn't feel that it was just – the pair had worked hard, had contributed a great deal and were receiving no financial recognition for that. They weren't entitled to a bonus but they deserved one. She went to the head of the division and explained the situation to him. And he agreed and ensured that the pair received a bonus, not as much as those who had been on the project for the whole time, but still something. Now Claire didn't have to go to the head of the division – there was nothing in it for her. It's a living example of how Paul encouraged the Philippians to live: 'In humility value others above yourselves, not looking to your own interests but each of you to the interests of the others' (Philippians 2:3–4).

So, you can be a mouthpiece for truth and justice, for fair dealing and right living, by speaking biblical wisdom into a situation, as June did. You can be a mouthpiece for truth and justice by suggesting to your rugby club that they buy fair-trade coffee, or by writing to your MP about the proposed bypass, or by emailing a TV channel about the demeaning portrayal of women in a particular programme, or by suggesting to your supermarket that they shouldn't sell soft-porn novels . . .

People might not be as attentive as the toy store owner or the university tutor. They might not pay any attention the first time or the second time or the third time. But things do change – whether it's the abolition of slavery, or the removal of kiddy sweets from near the tills, putting pornographic magazines on higher shelves in the newsagents, stopping football teams changing the design of their shirts more than once a season, cancelling the debt of severely indebted nations . . . Similarly, all of us over forty can remember a time when pretty much no-one recycled anything, and nutters in floppy, hand-knitted sweaters and cheesecloth skirts or orange flares wandered around like latter-day hippies enjoining us to save the planet . . . And then it began – people started recycling clear glass bottles, and then it was brown and green glass, and then cans. And now we've got plastic bins outside our houses for pretty much everything from aerosols to toenails. We're all nutters now. Change can take time. But good change is worth persevering for.

I wonder, where is there untruth and injustice on your frontline? And is there something for you to say with grace and courage?

May the Lord give you wisdom to know what and when and how.

## A prayer for this moment

Father,
help me to love mercy,
seek justice and walk humbly before you
on my frontline.
Give me ears to discern where falsehoods reign,
eyes to see where injustice has its roots,
wisdom and courage to cultivate truth and justice.
For your glory may it be.
Amen

## Questions for reflection

What unfairness or injustice or falsehoods do you see on your frontline?

In what ways might you respond?

Who might help?

## Exploring further

David Augsburger, *Caring Enough to Confront: How to Understand and Express Your Deepest Feelings Toward Others* (Ventura: Regal Books, 2009).

Guy Brandon, *Free to Live: Expressing the Love of Christ in an Age of Debt* (London: SPCK, 2010).

Timothy Keller, *Generous Justice: How God's Grace Makes Us Just* (London: Hodder & Stoughton, 2012).

Bob Roberts, Jr, *Real-Time Connections: Linking Your Job with God's Global Work* (Grand Rapids: Zondervan, 2010).

Amy L. Sherman, *Kingdom Calling: Vocational Stewardship for the Common Good* (Downers Grove: IVP, 2011).

Blessed are those who have learned to acclaim you . . .

Psalm 89:15

# 9.

## M6: BEING A MESSENGER OF THE GOSPEL

*Every day is an opportunity.*

A month ago, I felt drawn to pray for a particular friend, someone I'd prayed for on and off for a couple of years. The following day, there he is arriving at the Tube station at exactly the same time as I do. It happens very rarely indeed. It could be coincidence, but it feels like an answer to prayer. We travel in together and talk about one of the many things he knows about: Roman history. I learn a lot among other things that centurions don't command a hundred men, but eighty divided into groups of eight who share a tent, a servant to look after them and a mule to carry the tent and the cooking utensils.

Two weeks later, there's a men's conference at my church, and I hear that he might like to come. I text that if he's up for it, I am too. It's a good day – and we get to talk about our reactions to what the speakers have to say. More significantly, about two thirds of the way through, he tells me exactly where he stands in relation to God. He'd like to believe but he just doesn't. I don't happen to have a *'here's-one-I-prepared-earlier response' on the tip of my tongue, or indeed on any part of my tongue, but he has trusted me and actually I feel honoured by that. And now I know how to pray. And I'm encouraged to do so. After all, God is on the move.*

*He always is.*

As we have seen, there are all kinds of ways we demonstrate the difference Jesus makes in our lives and all kinds of ways we can serve people through our actions, but the people on our frontline also need to *hear* that it was Jesus who made the difference to us and that Jesus is the only one who can make an eternal difference to them. Jesus, after all, did not come only to serve and bless and heal people; he came 'to give his life as a ransom for many' (Mark 10:45). He wants to see people come to know him. But, as Paul puts it, '. . . how can they believe in the one of whom they have not heard?' (Romans 10:14).

So the question is: how can you be a messenger of the gospel on your particular frontline?

Don's* a Scot who lives in a suburb outside Glasgow. Still, as far as one of his frontlines is concerned, it wouldn't make any difference if he lived in a palm tree on an atoll in the South Pacific – as long as the phone worked. Don's frontline is his phone, specifically the people who call him at home trying to sell him mobile phone packages, electricity, double glazing. Most of us, I suspect, find these calls excruciatingly irritating, and we desperately try to find polite ways to get the sales-person off our phone so we can scurry back to our interrupted conversation or our child's homework or our burning dinner or the Wimbledon tie-break. Not Don. The call comes in: 'Do you have a mobile phone, Sir, and would you like to save money on your bills?' To which, Don replies something like this: 'I do, and would you like to hear about Jesus?' And, as he said to me, 'I'm not even paying for the call.' A true Scot indeed.

Of course, we can all learn something from Don's splendidly opportunistic ministry to people he is unlikely ever to meet, but for most of us, our main ministry is to people we're quite likely to see again. And, for most of us, evangelism is like a trip to the dentist's: we know we are meant to go, and when we get there we know we are meant to open our mouths, but we are rather afraid that when we do, extremely unpleasant and painful things will happen to us.

Interestingly, given a choice between evangelism and a dental appointment, many of us would rather go to the dentist. Why might we have a negative attitude to evangelism? There are probably a host of reasons, but I am rather convinced that this is primarily because we have a false view of what everyday evangelism is. Suppose that God does not actually expect many of us to have the eloquence of a great platform evangelist or the intellectual acuity of a university apologist. Suppose he just wants you to be able to 'give the reason for the hope that you have' (1 Peter 3:15). Suppose 'everyday evangelism' is our obedience to the Holy Spirit's promptings to draw alongside individuals he already knows and loves and is already working in.

Certainly, we can base our evangelism on three safe assumptions:

1. God wants people saved.
2. God is the lead evangelist – not you, not your pastor, not the DVD.
3. You have some role in this – however small.

Of course, every frontline is different. The people are different, the dynamics are different. Some contexts are downright hostile to the gospel, some are indifferent, some are open. Every frontline is a foreign country and they are all different. But whatever the frontline, we have some things going for us: we are there. God is with us. And we have time on our side.

Precisely because our frontline is a context we are in relatively frequently, we don't need to feel pressured to pull out the megaphone at the school gate and start preaching, nor type up an email with the word 'REPENT' in capitals in the subject line, address it to All Staff and press 'send', nor do we have to put ourselves under any daily pressure. God is always at work, and even if two seconds after someone asks you why you believe in Jesus, the phone rings, the baby wails, their bus arrives . . . well, there will probably be another moment, if not with you, then with another of God's messengers.

## Preparation and spontaneity

God is at work, so we don't need to be anxious and we certainly don't need to be driven. But we do need to be intentional. So, instead of worrying about what may or may not be 'appropriate' on our frontline, instead of being concerned that we are responsible for the evangelization of our entire family, our entire street, the whole company, the city of Bangalore – though who knows how God may work through us – let's begin by reminding ourselves that the Holy Spirit is at work and has, over many millennia, shown himself to be more than capable of overcoming a billion apparent obstacles to the communication of the good news in a myriad different contexts – open, closed and deliberately murderous.

Of course, there is a danger in trying to systematize anything as mysterious as evangelism, a danger in reducing it to ten principles or seven keys, or indeed the four steps I'm going to offer, as if there is a magic formula. It smacks of manipulation. And that is something to be wary of. Nevertheless, when we are learning something, it can be helpful to have a framework. Ultimately, it gives us freedom.

## Strictly go sharing

I love to dance. Though my children prefer it when I don't. Most of what I loosely call 'dancing' is what a generous friend might creatively dub 'improvised free movement' and what *Strictly Come Dancing*'s Craig Revel Horwood would have absolutely no words for at all. But I do actually sort of know how to do one proper dance with a partner. I know the basic steps – and they are basic – and I have a variety of moves that I can deploy. Now, if you have ever learned a dance, you'll know that, to begin with, unless you are very talented, you are brow-furrowed, eyes-down, focused on getting your feet in the right place on the right beat. To begin with, it's usually stilted, clumsy, self-conscious and embarrassing. However, when you know the steps, when you're no longer thinking about the steps, then you are free to express yourself, and it's flowing, liberated, unselfconscious and, in my case, still deeply embarrassing.

So here are four steps:

1. Praying for a particular person
2. Caring
3. Sharing truth
4. Offering paths forward

We'll look at prayer and care only briefly, because we've already seen their importance as we considered the other Ms.

So in this chapter we'll focus primarily on sharing the truth of the gospel and helping others explore further.

## 1. Praying for a particular person

It's often helpful when we're thinking about our part in God's work in people's lives to begin by asking him whether there's a particular person whom he might be wanting us to reach out to – in however small a way. Certainly, God may open up all kinds of opportunities with people we aren't praying for or perhaps have never met before. So, for example, an angel tells Philip to take the Gaza road out of Jerusalem and then to talk to the Ethiopian official reading Isaiah (Acts 8:26–40). The Gospels and the book of Acts are brimming with stories of significant encounters with strangers. Pray for those too. But it's important to consider the people God gives us regular opportunities to engage with.

Maybe someone comes to mind. Maybe you might pause and pray now: 'Lord, is there someone whose salvation you want me to be particularly concerned about? Please show me.'

You might be surprised. You might be horrified: 'Of all the people, in all the places I go to, it had to be her. Oh, Lord, you CANNOT be serious.'

Still, once you have a sense of who is on God's heart for you, you have a place to begin.

You can pray.

You can ask others to pray.

Prayer opens up the lines of communication between you and God about that person's salvation. You ask God to help you to genuinely love them, to genuinely want the very best for them, to understand them, appreciate them: that preening bodybuilder, that absolutely delightful boss, that awkward resident, that shy dog-walker with that perfectly groomed, muzzle-in-the-air miniature poodle, with its pink, faux-diamond studded collar and the topknot with a matching pink band.

## 2. Caring

So you pray for the person's salvation and you pray about how you might minister love and grace to them, how you can care for them. You can think about what interests them, what particular concerns they might have, what particular questions they might have or which of your Christian friends they might really get on with.

In sum, you can ask God how to develop the kind of open relationship that will allow you to get to know them, and them to get to know you. Evangelism does not always require deep friendship, nor does it necessarily lead to close friendship, but it does seem to me to require a kind of hospitable spirit – a desire to create a relationship where the other person feels safe. Sometimes I think I am too worried about me feeling comfortable to share, rather than being concerned that the other person feels comfortable being open with me, feels that I can be trusted, feels that they are safe.

Trust grows in a whole variety of ways. It grows as we live out the other Ms – as people see our character, see how we treat others with grace and love and how we care about them, even in incidental encounters.

### Of car parks and car boots
Anita used to work for a large company and, from time to time, as she walked the corridors, she'd walk past a colleague

from another department, whose name she did not know, and whose job she could only guess at, and she'd smile. The other woman would smile in return. Occasionally, a little hello would accompany the smile, but they had no occasion to pause or chat, for both had work to do. And so, time passed, counted in small smiles and little hellos.

And so it was that at the end of a day like any other, Anita was walking to her car in the company car park, and there coming towards her was the woman. The woman stopped and they began to talk. And she told Anita that her child was chronically ill with asthma and eczema and that she wanted to leave her husband. Anita listened and asked if she could pray for her and if her home group could pray for her child. And the woman said 'yes'. And Anita offered her a Bible from the box of Bibles in the boot of her car.

And afterwards, Anita prayed. And her home group prayed.

The child got a lot better, and the woman, who we shall call Sophia, did not leave her husband, but drew close to Christ and is now part of a local church.

And it began with a smile.

And I suspect that Anita smiled at lots of other people as she passed them in the corridor just as naturally, just as warmly. She wasn't 'trying' to develop a relationship, but she was open, aware of the other person, not self-absorbed. But it was only a smile. And somehow God worked through it to create the kind of trust that leads a woman in pain to share her life with a semi-stranger in the same office, to make herself vulnerable to rejection, to gossip, to humiliation.

Of course, Anita was ready in all kinds of ways: she knew what to say, she had Bibles in her boot and a home group she could turn to for prayer, but what was the trigger for that remarkable encounter? A smile in a corridor.

And what of God's hand?

Well, God so loved Sophia that, at her point of despair, it just so happened that she found herself in the same part of the car park as the person whom he had placed strategically in that workplace, just as he placed Queen Esther in the emperor's palace in Susa for such a time as that (Esther 4:14).

God loves the world.

God loves the people on your frontline.

So we pray for God to show us how we might deepen trust between us and the person we are praying for. We ask God to open a door not just for a gospel-focused conversation, but for a relationship of openness and trust. And, like Anita, we seek to be prepared for the encounters we are praying for, and indeed for the ones we don't expect.

## 3. Sharing truth

Part of being serious about wanting to see someone come to know Jesus is getting ready to share the good news with them. But here I am not talking about sharing a pre-packaged summary of how to become a Christian – though I have certainly found such summaries helpful to people who don't know Jesus. The gospel is more than a message about how to receive Jesus. The gospel, as we saw in chapter 3, includes the reality that Jesus' death and resurrection ushered in a new era in human history, created new possibilities for every human being's relationship with God and set out a dynamic vision for how to live in step with Christ. The gospel affects how we see everything. The gospel affects how we think about the news and film and sport and health and clothes and cosmetics and dance and orange-beaked toucans. The gospel affects how we see every situation and every person. No situation is outside God's care and no person is beyond his love. So, there are almost limitless opportunities to share gospel truth in ordinary conversations, some subtle like talking about 'creation' instead of 'mother nature', some more direct. Overall, though, I think there are three main ways in which we can bring the gospel into conversation:

1. Offering biblical perspectives on what's being talked about – films, family, football, finance . . .
2. Telling your stories about the ways Jesus has made, and continues to make, a difference to your life – personal testimony is compelling
3. Explaining the good news – finding helpful ways to communicate the invitation to a new way of life with Jesus

### Offering biblical perspectives

All kinds of things come up in conversation. And the question is: how can we find natural gospel ways to talk about things that other people already want to talk about, not just ways to talk about what *we* want to talk about?

The goal is not to crowbar an evangelistic opportunity into the conversation:

'What a lovely day,' she said, closing her eyes as she tilted her head like a giant sunflower up towards the radiant orb.

'Yes,' he replied, 'it was just like this the day I found Jesus.'

No, the goal is not to manufacture an opportunity to speak out the gospel and then heave a sigh of relief as all our pent-up guilt thuds to the floor. It's not as if we are a hunter stalking a deer, manoeuvring ourselves stealthily into position, making sure the conditions are just right – the wind, the ground cover, the distance – waiting for that one moment to get that shot off – and that done, all is done. Rather, we are seeking to invite a fellow human being created in the image of God into a continuing conversation about Jesus.

And in the best conversations, people are honest.

Not many of us breeze through life with a cherubic smile, our fountain of ebullience untouched by disappointment, illness, grief, self-doubt, redundancy, unrequited love or getting a parking ticket when we just popped in for a paper. And it really is unhelpful to pretend otherwise. Giving others our trust is vital if we want theirs, so it's always best to be open and honest about where we really are and what our experience with God has really been like.

And in the best conversations, people ask questions.

In the best conversations, people try to find out what the other person thinks. When the rich young man asks Jesus, 'Teacher, what good thing must I do to get eternal life?' Jesus doesn't answer immediately. He first asks him a question so he can discern the man's spiritual state and therefore answer the question more helpfully (Matthew 19:16–21). Of course, we don't ask questions to expose people's comparative lack of knowledge about Christianity or to make them aware how little they've actually thought about life's bigger questions – we might in fact be rather surprised. We ask in order to understand where they're at, to find out what they believe and why.

Indeed, in the best conversations, people listen. 'Everyone should be quick to listen, slow to speak and slow to become angry,' says James (1:19).

Being listened to, being properly heard, is an amazing gift in itself. As David Augsburger said, 'Being heard is so close to being loved, that for the average person they are almost indistinguishable.'[1] Sometimes, however, there's a danger that we are so concerned to say what we want to say that we don't take the time to listen carefully, to try to understand the other person and appreciate them. This doesn't mean we go prying into their private lives; rather it means that we are interested in how they see things.

A conversation about an incident in a favourite soap opera can become an opportunity to talk about what they think the characters should have done or what you might have done and why. Indeed, TV programmes and films are brimming with relational issues that can easily lead to conversations that allow you to offer a biblical perspective. How, for example, can a husband forgive the man who has raped his wife? Where will he get the power to do that? What happens to us when we don't forgive?

Similarly, a conversation about football (you may not be able to avoid it) can become an opportunity to rejoice in the wondrous and sometimes improbable skill that God has created in human beings, to comment on character, or to reflect not just on a team's success but its values. Or perhaps it becomes an opportunity to think about how we respond to justice and injustice in refereeing decisions, or to explore the balance between a player's loyalty to a team and their desire to test themselves at a higher level, or to consider how greed, or perhaps an inflated view of their own ability, leads talented players to leave for bigger clubs, only to find themselves hardly playing at all.

I'm not saying it's easy. We may not yet be that good at bringing biblical perspectives to bear on such matters, but maybe that's not a bad thing to learn. It enriches our appreciation of the world around us.

Of course, we may not have that much in common with the people we meet, or even the particular person God is prompting us to pray for. But if God is calling us to reach out to them, then we should seek to meet them on their ground, to try to understand their world, just as an overseas missionary would work hard to understand the language and culture of the land God is sending them to, or a hopeful suitor might look up a few Finnish phrases to impress that alluring woman from Helsinki (I did. I'm not sure she was that impressed – probably thought I was a bit desperate – but she married me anyway).

We meet others on their ground. So we seek to bring gospel perspectives to the general things people talk about and to the personal things people talk about: the tutor who fancies them, the child who is being difficult, the worry over a parent, the boss they can't deal with, the boyfriend they're not sure about . . .

People are craving wisdom for their lives. And God has built a lot of wisdom into you already through your life experience, through parents and teachers, through your own Bible reading, through preachers and friends. People don't have to agree with you – it's just your point of view – but a grain of truth is more valuable than a ton of chaff.

Still, people need to hear more than gospel perspectives on issues they are facing; they need to hear what Jesus has done for us and them and the kind of life he invites them to lead.

### Telling your stories

The apostle Peter writes: 'Always be prepared to give an answer to everyone who asks you to give the reason for the hope that you have' (1 Peter 3:15).

Notice Peter doesn't say, 'Always be prepared to answer any and every difficult question someone might lob at you.'

Rather, he says, 'Be prepared to give an answer to everyone who asks you to give the reason for the hope that *you* have.'

The word 'reason' here is not, I believe, limited to logical argument, as if the only 'reason' we follow Jesus is because we are intellectually convinced by the arguments for his resurrection, his divinity and his sovereign claim on every aspect of our lives. Certainly, intellectual reasons for trusting in God are vital. So, for example, when Paul stands before Agrippa, he makes the case for Jesus' messiahship based on Agrippa's understanding of 'all the Jewish customs and controversies' (Acts 26:3). Paul, however, also communicates his experience of God's action in his own life (Acts 26:12–22). There is a time to persuade, a time to tell your story and a time for both.

Why do *you* follow Jesus? Yes, because you believe he is who he says he is. He is the truth. But he is also the way and the life. And we are to testify to this too. So, for example, after the demon-possessed Legion is healed, he begs Jesus to let him go with him, but Jesus says, 'Return home and tell how much God has done for you' (Luke 8:39). Similarly, in the case of the Samaritan woman, her fellow-villagers come out to meet Jesus by the well, because she has told them, 'Come, see a man who told me everything I've ever done. Could this be the Messiah?' (John 4:29) And they believe in him 'because of the woman's testimony' (John 4:39).

What has the Lord done for you?

He has loved me beyond my imagining. He took my mess and gave me his mercy. He took my sin and gave me his Son. He died for me and I don't have to do anything to earn his love. He forgave my sinful rebellion against him and he forgives my daily sins. He has guaranteed me a place in his house. He is with me. Now and forever. And that's just for starters . . . He gave me the Holy Spirit. And on one extra-ordinary afternoon in a Chicago church, his presence came upon me and gave me a deep sense of assurance of his love that has never left me. He listens to me. And he speaks to me through his Word. He's brought good, wise, joy-bringing friends into my life. He healed me. He gave me a taste for purity. And sustained me when my heart was broken. He gave me a higher purpose in and through the work I did in advertising. He helped me get through when things were really tough. He helped my family get through when things were really tough. He helped us when money was tight . . .

And last Sunday he spoke to me about kindness, and someone who didn't know that came over to me and prayed over me about kindness. And just yesterday I met my historian friend on the Tube on the way home, and we talked about Roman tax collectors and about atheism and an address I'd heard by John Lennox, a Christian professor of mathematics, and I mentioned that I might have a book at home by him, and he said he'd like to read it. And I found it – which is not as easy as it sounds. And passed it on to him that evening . . . And this very Wednesday morning I was reading 1 John, and there was something in there for my family at this time . . . God in the big things and God in the little big things. He is alive.

What has the Lord done for you? I wonder what comes to mind.

Because the more that comes to mind, the more aware we are of what God has done, the easier it is for us to testify to others about his action in our lives and the wonder of who he is.

What has the Lord done for you? What will he do? What is he doing?

Just suppose, for example, you're in a difficult situation with someone, and somehow God's peace and presence have prevented you from exploding, and then a friend or colleague says something like: 'I just do not understand how you can be so calm in your situation. I'd have murdered him.'

'Well,' you reply, 'I wanted to. Actually, I was absolutely Vesuvian with anger, so flaming furious that it would have made Gordon Ramsay look like Mary Poppins, but in the midst of it I suddenly found myself praying for him. Or at

least, asking God to help me to pray for him. And I asked a
friend to do the same . . . And I began to wonder, why had he
done such a thing? What fear or bitterness or resentment had
triggered it? And I remember a week after he did it, I was
reading my Bible and this sentence just popped out at me like
a flashing neon sign: "Love your enemies." And it hit me. I'd
never thought of having enemies before, but he was my
enemy – he'd done me a lot of damage. And I was to love *him*.
Him? God's timing was brilliant. If I'd read that verse the
day after he'd done it, I probably wouldn't have been able to
even take it in. So I asked God to help me love him, forgive
him . . . The volcano is still simmering, I'm afraid. Smoke still
rises, but every week I find my attitude changing. Prayer
works.'

In sum, one of the ways we can be a messenger of the
gospel is by celebrating and testifying to how Jesus has been
at work in our lives. In such situations, it's important to give
God the credit, just as Daniel does when Nebuchadnezzar asks
him about his ability to interpret dreams.

*Revealing your sources*
Daniel has graduated from Imperial College Babylon, the best
university in the magnificent capital of the most powerful
empire on earth, and he is now a senior civil servant. The
emperor, Nebuchadnezzar, the most powerful man in the
world, has a disturbing dream and commands his magicians
and sorcerers and advisors to interpret it. He, however, refuses
to tell them what the dream was, though he does offer them
a significant incentive to succeed – their lives. Interpret or die.
Now it is rather difficult to interpret a dream that you know
nothing about. Still, from Nebuchadnezzar's point of view,
this should not be an obstacle, since his magicians and
sorcerers do claim to have access to the wisdom of the gods.

Daniel, as you may recall, goes to Nebuchadnezzar and asks for a little time. He then asks Hananiah, Mishael and Azariah to pray. Their names are perhaps significant here, meaning respectively: 'God is gracious', 'Who is like God?' and 'God helps'. God does indeed show himself to be gracious. He does what only he could do, and helps by revealing the dream and its interpretation to Daniel. So Daniel goes to Nebuchadnezzar to give him the interpretation of the dream that Nebuchadnezzar has told no-one about and cannot understand. At this point, Daniel could say to Nebuchadnezzar, 'No wise man, enchanter, magician or diviner can explain to the king the mystery he has asked about . . . *except me.*'

But he doesn't. He says this:

> No wise man, enchanter, magician or diviner can explain to the king the mystery he has asked about, but there is a God in heaven who reveals mysteries. He has shown King Nebuchadnezzar what will happen in days to come.
> (Daniel 2:27–28)

He gives the credit to God.

Someone at the gym tells you that their daughter's having trouble with her marriage, and you say, 'Well, my husband and I went through a tough time, but people prayed for us, I prayed for us, and I got some good practical advice from this course I went on at a local church. It's still not perfect – but hey, better than meltdown.'

Of course, being ready to give a reason is not just about the content of the message; it's also about how to say it. I don't think Peter meant, 'Always be prepared to drop some pre-packaged, rehearsed formulaic summary of the gospel into the conversation.' I think he meant, 'Always be prepared to answer the question in a way that is true to you and appropriate to the person asking you.' After all, when Jesus meets Nicodemus (John 3), a highly respectable, highly educated Jewish rabbi who seems rather slow to understand who Jesus is, he doesn't talk to him in the same way that he talks to the much-divorced, no doubt ill-educated Samaritan woman at the well in Samaria who is actually rather quick to recognize who he really is.

### Explaining the good news

So, having explored how we might salt our conversation with biblical perspectives, and how we might testify to the differ-ence that Jesus makes in our lives, we look now at how we might prepare ourselves to explain what Jesus has done and the life he invites us into.

And this should be one of our hopes and goals. But are we ready to do it?

Many people don't feel that they are.

They don't feel that they have a way of explaining the gospel that will actually communicate with the people they meet. Part of this may be that some of the ways we have been taught do seem formulaic, seem made for a formal presen-tation, not an informal conversation. Part of the solution may be that we simply need to practise a bit.

It's a curious thing. After I was taught how to share the story of how I became a Christian in under five minutes without using any Christian jargon, I seemed to have a lot of oppor-tunities to do just that. I don't suppose I ever told it the same way, and I'm sure that when I tell it, I tailor it to the person I'm talking to, but the preparation helped enormously.

Similarly, once I had learned how to share a simple gospel presentation, it was rather extraordinary how much more often I seemed to get an opportunity to use it, or parts of it, in a conversation. The more tools you have, the more opportunities seem to present themselves. Preparation not only enables us to take opportunities; it helps us to see them.

But that doesn't mean that opportunities don't come unless we are really well prepared. They do.

God will work through the knowledge you have right now. However, where we are right now is not necessarily where he would like us to be in a year's time or two years' time. Right now, I might not be in a position to answer some of the questions the people I'm concerned about might ask me. Indeed, I've no doubt that, though I could give my history-loving friend a reason for the hope that is in me, there's a phalanx of questions that he could ask me tomorrow on the Tube to which I wouldn't have a helpful response. But where might I be in a year's time or two years' time? Similarly, if someone does pose a question you don't have a response to, well, it's OK to say, 'Good question. I've never really thought about that. I'll rootle around and get back to you on that.' And then do so.

Quite apart from anything else, other people's questions are opportunities to grow deeper in our understanding of Christ. Indeed, God may be using them to help us grow closer to him. And, as I said before, we don't have to win the argument. Paul doesn't persuade King Agrippa (Acts 26), but he does communicate the gospel.

Indeed, while we yearn for people to become followers of Jesus, they don't always respond the way we would like. Here's another story about my friend Anita.

*Taking a dive*
'You should try it – it's fantastic,' enthused Anita's skydiver colleague, as she waxed lyrical about the joys of jumping out of an aeroplane with nothing but a few pieces of string and a couple of silk handkerchiefs between you and an early entry to heaven. 'If you come to church, I'll go skydiving,' said

Anita. Not a bad swap, you might think, but Anita's colleague decided that going to church was too great a sacrifice to make in the attempt to convert another landlubber to the pleasures of terminal velocity.

A year passed and once again Anita found herself listening to her colleague extolling the virtues of skydiving: 'You should try it.'

'I told you,' Anita said, 'you come to church and I'll go skydiving.'

'Why do you want me to come to church?'

'Well,' said Anita, 'you want me to go skydiving because you think it's a fantastic experience. I want you to come to church because knowing Jesus is a fantastic experience.' A pretty clear testimony.

Her colleague went to church. And in due course Anita jumped out of an aeroplane. It's not clear who thought they were being braver. But it certainly cost Anita more – £375 for the training, the jump and the photos. Entrepreneurially, Anita decided to do a sponsored jump, turning over all the proceeds of her high-altitude leap to a Christian charity working with the poor. Curiously, after the jump, her relationship with her colleague took almost as spectacular a dive as Anita had taken – except there was no parachute. Eventually Anita asked her why. 'You're too nice. I don't know what it is, but I just don't like you.'

Prayer, initiative, verbal witness, financial investment and a fair dollop of courage – but in terms of her colleague's journey towards Christ, things looked worse than before. Success or failure?

That depends on whose job you think it is to convert people.

Agape, the global mission organization, have a wonderful definition of successful witnessing: 'Taking the initiative to share the gospel in the power of the Holy Spirit and leaving the results to God.'

We do our bit. God does his. In his time.

## 4. Offering paths forward

So, as messengers of the gospel, we seek to be intentional about praying, intentional about taking initiative to develop relationships, and intentional about being prepared to speak. And we rely on God. The disciples, for example, after Peter and John's imprisonment, and their early release for worshipful behaviour, gather and pray for the mission:

> Now, Lord, consider their threats and enable your servants to speak your word with great boldness. Stretch out your hand to heal and perform signs and wonders through the name of your holy servant Jesus.
>
> (Acts 4:29)

They pray for God to enable them to continue to be faithful to the mission he has given them, so they pray for boldness to speak and for God to show his power in miraculous ways. I wonder if we might pray for both for our frontline.

Beyond that, we might ask ourselves what the next steps might be for the person we are concerned about?

Two of the main ways the Lord chooses to draw people to himself are through his Word and through his people.

So, could you invite someone to read the Bible together in a coffee shop, or to an explorer's course? Or could you give them a photocopy of a psalm or a little card with a Bible verse on it? Anita had a box of Bibles in her boot, presumably because she expected to have an opportunity to give them away. I wonder what material we might have on hand to give away that helps people on the next step.

Perhaps your frontline is a place where you meet lots of strangers. For two particular ladies, their frontline is a bench in a shopping centre where they wait to see who God brings to sit next to them. Well, if your frontline is like that, maybe you might have a few little olive crosses in your pocket like Peter the litter-picker, or a little card with the name of your church as one midwife suggested, or a pen and paper to write down a phone number.

As for involving other Christians, you may be alone on your frontline, but that does not mean you need to be engaged in mission alone. I wonder, is there another Christian you think your person might enjoy meeting, who shares their enthusiasm for war-gaming or the hits of Herman's Hermits or miniature poodles? Is there a social event you could invite them to? A barbecue, a quiz evening, a 'blokey-blokes' weekend with beer and bacon in a soggy field, a party, a cupcake-making fest in your kitchen, a book club?

The interesting thing is that the more we actually expect God to act on our frontline, the more important the body of Christ becomes. If I expect people to be interested in the gospel and my frontline is the local school, then it may really matter to me that I feel I could invite someone to something in my church community, whether it's a social event or a service. If I expect God to act in someone else's life, it becomes more important that I can find someone who may be able to help me answer the questions I don't feel I can answer, or to be the person who can come alongside them where they live. Frontliners need back-up.

And in many situations frontliners need perseverance.

The good news is that God made human beings for relationship with him – we aren't trying to convert an ox into a

gazelle, but to see a human being created to follow Jesus transformed into a Jesus-following human being. It usually takes
time, and we may not see the results ourselves. So we pray,
we listen, we seek to bless people, to develop relationships,
and we seek to grow in knowledge and understanding of the
gospel, speaking out gospel truth as the Spirit gives opportunity, and we trust in the God who is infinitely creative and
is not willing that any should perish.

Oh, and I've just found out that my friend is going to an
explorer's course.

God is on the move.

Exciting, isn't it?

### A prayer for this moment

Father, thank you for saving me.
Thank you that I can call you Father
because of what your Son has done for me.
Thank you for all those who showed and shared
your good news with me.
Father, draw all those on my frontline to your Son,
stretch out your mighty hand to do great works there
and give me wisdom and boldness in word and deed
to show and share your way to life.
For your glory may it be.
Amen.

**Praying for a particular person? Some questions.**

Here are a few questions to consider. You may not
know all the answers. Indeed, it's often amazing how
little we sometimes know about people we spend quite
a bit of time with.

Family / life stage / occupation?

Hobbies / enthusiasms / favourites / main interests?

What are their goals / hopes / dreams? What's
important to them?

What are their beliefs? What do you think they think
of Christianity?

What particular blessings could you pray for them?

What do you particularly like / enjoy about them?

What do you dislike / find difficult about them?

What might you do to serve, help, honour, encourage them and develop your relationship?

## Exploring further

John Chapman, *Know and Tell the Gospel* (New Malden:
  The Good Book Company, 1998).
Michael Green, *Compelled by Joy: A Lifelong Passion for
  Evangelism* (Nottingham: IVP, 2011).
David Male and Paul Weston, *The Word's Out: Speaking the
  Gospel Today* (Abingdon: BRF, 2013).
J. Mack Stiles, *Marks of the Messenger: Knowing, Living and
  Speaking the Gospel* (Downers Grove: IVP, 2010).
Andrew P. Wilson, *If God, Then What? Wondering Aloud about
  Truth, Origins and Redemption* (Nottingham: IVP, 2012).

Olive crosses can be purchased from Bob Whittle:
bobwhittle@btinternet.com.

## Note
 1. David Augsburger, *Caring Enough to Hear and Be Heard* (Regal
    Books, 1982), p. 12.

# GROWING IN FRUITFULNESS

He has made everything beautiful in its time.

Ecclesiastes 3:11

# 10.

# THE GARDENER'S TALE

I am the true vine, and my Father is the gardener.
He cuts off every branch in me that bears no fruit,
while every branch that does bear fruit he prunes
so that it will be even more fruitful.

ABIDE IN ME

John 15:1–2

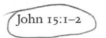

It was Monday morning, February, and very cold. Judith arrived at school to discover that the heating had broken and several hundred children were about to arrive. On a very cold February Monday.

She was the head teacher and there was already plenty in her diary before the boiler broke. But that's how her day began — figuring out a way to get enough heaters in the classrooms to keep the school open. And fast.

And her day ended with a very angry child making things very difficult, a troublesome child who'd been troublesome rather too often before. And so, reluctantly, she found herself having to exclude him. It's not something any head likes to do. That was how her day ended. Not the bestest of days on her frontline.

But when she got home, after what was a really rather grim day, after a day when she might well have been justified in having a mega-whinge, or soothing herself with a glass or two of medicinal wine

*or a large tub of quadruple chocolate ice cream, something strange*
*happened. As she put it, 'I found myself thanking God for trusting*
*me with all that.'*

*God trusted her with it, as God trusted Moses with the Israelites.*
*These were the people God had given her to love. These were the*
*challenges he was expecting her to handle – with him.*

*God is trusting us with our frontlines, trusting us with the people*
*there, trusting us with the challenges there, trusting us with the*
*tasks there, trusting us to be his people there. A privilege really, an*
*honour.*

There have been a lot of true stories in this book, stories of
people of different ages and different backgrounds, some from
the Bible, some alive today. They are all stories about people
who have seen the places where they spend time differently,
seen that they can love God doing whatever they do, seen the
people on their frontlines differently, and seen that they can,
by God's grace, be fruitful for him where they already spend
time. God with them.

We've looked at fruitfulness through six lenses and also
recognized it's not quite as neat as that. The Ms are inevitably
interconnected: godly character leads to godly action. And
godly character or godly action or speaking up for truth or
moulding culture can all prompt questions in others and
lead to the opportunity to explain the reason for the hope
that we have. Beyond that, all forms of fruitfulness have
their source in Christ, the vine, and in the sovereign tending
of the Father. And all forms of fruitfulness ultimately will
bring glory to his name and contribute to others seeing
a clearer and clearer picture of who he is. Praise God for
that.

The question for all of us is: how do we hold on to the
vision for the frontline, and carry on, go deeper, grow ever

more fruitful to his glory? Yes, as we saw in earlier chapters, there may be specific skills to learn or hone, and specific issues to explore but, though skill and knowledge are important, they do not in themselves bring life.

At its simplest, we grow for the frontline by integrating the frontline into the basic disciplines of the Christian life:

1. Our praying
2. Our fellowship with other Christians – the support we ask for, the questions we pose, the wisdom we seek, the conversations we initiate, and the encouragement we offer others
3. Our Bible reading

## 1. Attentive praying

What do you pray for?

The reality is that we are probably less in the habit of praying for the people and situations on our frontlines than we are for church-based activities. And that's perhaps because we don't hear many other people praying for their frontlines or hear many prayers in church for frontlines. But the Lord is no less interested in those situations, those people, or in you when you are there. Bring it all to the Lord in prayer.

Still, prayer, as we know, is more than making requests; it is a conversation with the Father, an opportunity to listen as well as to speak. So, for our frontlines, we not only make requests, we ask questions. We ask for God's perspective, we ask him to show us what he is doing, to reveal to us what he wants us to learn, what he wants us to do now . . . We seek to become more attentive to God. We listen.

### With David on the frontline?

There are many prayers in the Bible from a whole host of
figures – from Abraham to Moses to Jesus to Paul. However,
overall we probably have more examples of the prayer life of
David than of any other person. Indeed, both in the two books
of Samuel and in the Psalms, we are given an extraordinary
insight into the sheer range of issues that David prays about
– much of it in relation to the issues he faced on his frontline
– as soldier, general, fugitive and king.

We hear David calling out to God for protection from his
enemies. We hear David asking God for wisdom for big
decisions – whether or not, for example, to repel a Philistine
raiding party (2 Samuel 5:19). And we hear David being given
wisdom for the smaller issue of a battle plan (2 Samuel
5:23–24). But David's praying and singing are not just about
what he wants, but about his wonder and gratitude at the
evidence he sees of God's hand in every area and phase of his
life: his creation in the womb (Psalm 139), his training for
the job God had for him to do (Psalm 144:1), his protection
in battle (Psalm 18:3), his protection on the run (Psalm
18:47–48), his granting of peace and privilege (Psalm 16:5–8)
. . . David's praying reveals an alertness not only to God's
direction, but to God's provision and intervention. So we
come to God in prayer, not only to see what we might do, but
to be shown what God has done for us.

How is it that David escaped Saul all those years? How is it
that he never turned an ankle in all those years of fighting on
Israel's often rough and craggy terrain (Psalm 18:36)? How is
it that he had the courage to take on a troop (Psalm 18:29)?
How is it that all those enemies never got him? God. God
hears his cry. God stoops down from heaven: 'He parted the
heavens and came down' (Psalm 18:9), and 'He reached down
from on high and took hold of me' (Psalm 18:16).

David is aware that God wants to be involved in every aspect of his life and therefore he is confident to bring all to him in prayer. His confidence is in the God of All. And because he is confident in the God of All, he depends on God, he talks to God, is attentive to God, desires to please God, thanks God and gives glory to God.

Importantly, David's praying does not just happen at home, or in times of worship in Jerusalem; it happens on the frontline. And so we too might begin to find ways to pray for our frontlines on our frontlines. Yes, in moments of crisis, like Jehoshaphat crying out to God in the middle of battle (2 Chronicles 18:31) – help me with this teacher; give me wisdom with this guy who has had too much to drink at the Christmas bash; give me patience with this complaining customer . . . But prayer is not just for the crisis; we pray for the shalom, the peace and prosperity of our frontline, and the blessing and salvation of all those there.

So let us begin to pray more deliberately on our frontlines. You might walk round your frontline – the supermarket or gym or school – in silent prayer. Or simply pray there briefly, silently, every time you go there – an arrow prayer as you walk into the pub, the ward or into someone's home to fix their boiler. One woman decided to pray the Lord's Prayer at her desk before the start of her day for a week. It was so transformative that, last time I heard, she was on day 35 . . . Our frontlines are a context for prayer, for worship, for thanksgiving. And indeed, for involving others in prayer – both on our frontline and for our frontlines.

## 2. Fellowship for the frontline

If there is another Christian on your frontline, it's worth trying to get together, if you possibly can, to pray specifically for the issues and people there. Curiously, many workplace groups end up praying for everything but the actual workplace they're in and the people they spend time with – their pattern for prayer mimics the pattern common in many churches and home groups.

Indeed, you may or may not be part of a church that has grasped the importance of our daily frontlines. The impact of the sacred-secular divide has meant that many churches have limited their mission concerns to church-based local initiatives and overseas opportunities. Similarly, most small-group prayer times tend to focus on personal pressure points and crises – the relative who is ill, the child doing badly at school, the big meeting coming up – and it's right to pray for those needs. But it's rare to pray for our daily mission priorities on the frontline. It is rare for fellow-believers to know the name of the barman you are praying for, or your boss, or the checkout person who is on your heart . . . So, our praying in church, and especially in small groups and with prayer partners, should embrace not only crises, not only the projects we're involved in together in church, but our mission on our frontlines. We may go out onto our frontline alone physically, but we should not go without the prayer, wise advice and encouragement of other Christians.

Of course, you may not lead your home group and so be able to determine its overall priorities, but you can ask others for prayer for your frontline and you can ask how you might pray for theirs. You may not be in a church where the leaders are yet tuned in to this view of mission (perhaps give them a copy of *Imagine Church: Releasing Whole-Life Disciples* by Neil Hudson), but you could still invite one of your leaders to come to your frontline and pray for it, or ask them for wisdom for a particular situation. It will help you and it will help them.

And you could do the same with a prayer partner or someone from your home group.

You can perhaps begin to have a helpful impact on other areas of church life. You may not write the church prayer bulletin, but that doesn't stop you submitting requests that relate to the frontline. You may not lead the sung worship in your church, but you could perhaps suggest that the leader might include songs or prayers that include a concern for people's everyday contexts, or even a picture or two on the PowerPoint that suggest that God is not only to be found on lonely mountain tops or in glowing sunsets but also in city streets and industrial parks.

The reality is that there are many, many wonderful stories of what happens when a local church gets behind their overseas missionaries in prayer and wisdom and encouragement and finance, but we do not yet have many stories of what God does when a local church gets behind frontline missionaries in prayer and wisdom and encouragement and perhaps even in finance.

So we bring our frontlines to godly friends for wisdom, prayer and encouragement. And we bring the consciousness that God is concerned about every aspect of our lives to our reading of the Bible.

## 3. Reflecting on our frontline in our Bible reading

As we saw in chapter 3, the Bible is crystal clear that there is no aspect of our lives that God is not concerned about and no nook of the universe that is outside his care. And so we come to God's Word, bringing all of our life to him and seeking wisdom for all of our life from him. 2 Timothy 3:16–17 makes the connection between God's Word and godly living crystal clear: 'All Scripture is God-breathed and is useful for teaching, rebuking, correcting and training in righteousness, so that the servant of God may be thoroughly equipped for every good work.'

If we read the Bible with our frontlines in mind, this might stir us to wonder how the God we see acting in the Bible might act there. It might stir us to ask ourselves how the lessons God teaches his people there might apply to us, how we might find wisdom in Proverbs, or challenge in the character qualities affirmed in the Sermon on the Mount, or motivation to speak out against exploitation in the example of the prophets, or hope for justice in the book of Revelation.

If we read the Bible with our frontline in mind, then it might make us more attentive to what the Bible tells us about the particular contexts people find themselves in – Sarah in a nomadic culture and in the court of Pharaoh, Deborah, a judge in a patriarchal culture, Obadiah working for Ahab in idolatrous Israel, Ezekiel in imperial Babylon, Priscilla and Aquila in polytheistic and apparently invincible Rome, and so on . . . And perhaps we see how God has helped his people in very different contexts and we grow in confidence that he can help us in ours.

If we read the Bible with our frontline in mind, then it could make us more alert to the lessons we might learn from how God works through them. We began with the biblical account of a captive Israelite girl enslaved to an Aramite mistress and how God worked through her (2 Kings 5), but we could as easily have begun with a nomadic herdsman (Abraham) and his barren wife (Sarah) negotiating life in pagan societies (Genesis 12 – 23), or a serially oppressed teenage dreamer (Joseph) in slavery, in prison, in power (Genesis 37 – 50). Or we could have begun with an astute, decisive, courageous and verbally brilliant wife (Abigail) who intervenes to prevent an incensed David from killing her rich but boorish husband and plundering their property (1 Samuel 25).

The people we meet in the Bible are not Sunday-school cut-outs, but real people seeking to live out their lives in very varied conditions – there is something to learn from them and from the Lord who works in, through and sometimes despite them.

If we bring our frontlines to our reading of the Bible, perhaps too we will see our frontlines and our own lives in the framework of that bigger story that God is weaving.

## The 6M disciple in the bigger picture

So, for example, we might read the story of Boaz in the book of Ruth and reflect on him not only as an example of a whole-life 6M disciple on the frontline, but as a man unknowingly playing a role in God's longer-term plan.

We first meet Boaz as he arrives at his fields and greets his workers: 'The Lord be with you,' he says. He is the first believer in the one true God that the Bible records using that phrase. Today it is most often associated with Church of England priests who say it to their congregation inside a church, usually on a Sunday, sometimes wearing robes. Boaz, however, is not a priest; he's a farmer. And he says it outside, at work, on a working weekday, in his work clothes, and he's addressing his foreman and the men and women harvesting his crops.

'The Lord be with you.' It's a prayer that God might show them favour in this ordinary work, on this ordinary harvest day under the hot Bethlehem sun. 'The Lord be with you in your accounting'; 'The Lord be with you as you make an arrest'; 'The Lord be with you in this meeting'; 'The Lord be with you as you change a nappy'; 'The Lord be with you as you serve someone coffee'. Boaz is a godly man, seeking to do good work in God's way with God's power.

Of course, the phrase 'the Lord be with you' might just have been a conversational convention, just a way that people greeted one another, but there are clues in the text to suggest that, in Boaz's case, it's a greeting that reveals a genuine concern for his employees and a radical Godward orientation. Indeed, Boaz is introduced as 'a man of standing' (Ruth 2:1). It's the same Hebrew word Boaz himself uses to describe the communal perception of Ruth (3:11), so here it is not so much a reference to high status as to godly character.

Ruth is allowed to glean in Boaz's fields, and Boaz may feel he has to allow it because the Mosaic law tells him to (Leviticus 23:22), but he doesn't have to offer Ruth bread dipped in wine vinegar at lunchtime (the tenth-century BC equivalent of salt and vinegar crisps). He doesn't have to give her permission to drink from the water jars filled for his paid workers. He doesn't have to tell his harvesters to deliberately let some stalks fall so she can glean more grain. He doesn't have to pray for her. But he does. Boaz ministers grace and love.

Similarly, Boaz maintains a certain set of values that his men, he knows, will abide by – even though he doesn't have an Investors in People Kitemark. His corporate ethos works its way into his employees' behaviour. So, for example, Boaz tells Ruth not to glean in other people's fields, because in those she might be sexually harassed. Israel is, after all, in spiritual decline. Indeed, the narrator has clarified that the story takes place in the period of the Judges (1:1). Given that David's birth is only three generations away, it's clear that Israel had already seen several generations of the spiral of radical degeneration that was to lead to civil war. In Boaz's fields, however, godly standards still prevail. Ruth will be safe: 'I have told the men not to lay a hand on you' (Ruth 2:9). He is a mouthpiece of protective justice – and he is intentionally moulding a particular kind of workplace culture.

Boaz is impressive at work, but he is also impressive at play. He knows how to have a good time. After the barley harvest is in, he joins the party and is wise enough not to drink and ride his donkey, but kips down in the barn and sleeps it off.

Boaz is also remarkably self-controlled. Indeed, on several occasions the text makes it clear that he is significantly older than Ruth. Certainly, he is old enough to recognize that such a young woman might well not be interested in him, but he's still young enough to jump at the chance when it is clear that she is. In contemporary Britain that would make him somewhere between thirty and eighty-seven years old! Nevertheless, despite his long bachelorhood, Boaz does not rush in to clinch the deal, but respects the biblical law and ensures that the relative with a prior legal claim on Ruth's hand in marriage has first right of refusal. And he does this in a public place in the presence of the elders of the village, so that there can be no dispute about whether right has or has not been done. He may not have an opportunity to be a messenger of the gospel, but he does clearly take his opportunities to verbally express God's laws and his allegiance to them.

Again, it's important to see that legally Boaz doesn't *have* to do any of these things – except allow Ruth to glean. He certainly did not have to take any initiative to marry Ruth. He could have laid low and left the kinsman redeemer with a prior claim to find out about Ruth in his own good time. No, it's clear that Boaz wants to marry Ruth. He is a willing redeemer. Just as God did not *have to* rescue his people in the Judges period. Just as God did not *have to* send his Son. He did so because he wanted to. So did Boaz. Love and obedience are intertwined.

Overall, the picture we have of Boaz is of a believer who is dependent on God, concerned for his employees, generous to the needy, joyous in celebration, sexually pure and community minded. He's a man who models godly character, does good work, shows grace and love, creates a positive working culture, is committed to justice, and testifies to the primacy of God's laws over personal preference. A 6M disciple in deed and word and heart.

Indeed, Boaz shows us that being a disciple is more than being a good egg, more than showing integrity, more than speaking out the gospel as the Spirit leads; it is about concern for the poor and the marginalized, about godly structures and practices, about demonstrating that putting the values of the God and Father of our Lord Jesus at the heart of a frontline or a life might actually be good news. As indeed it is.

And we might stop there. But Boaz and Ruth are part of something much bigger. In Ruth 2:3, we read: 'As it turned out, she [Ruth] was working in a field belonging to Boaz, who was from the clan of Elimelek.' She didn't choose that field because she knew it belonged to a relative who was unmarried and wealthy and highly respected. It just happened. But equally, it's clear that God was in it. In this apparent coincidence, in this happy meeting between a man and a younger woman, in the to-ings and fro-ings of normal everyday life, in their marriage and the gift of a child that Ruth gives to her mother-in-law to care for . . . An everyday story really.

But this poor, young Moabite widow who just happened to go gleaning for grain in this man's Bethlehem fields less than ten miles from the town that would become the City of David, this woman and this man are the great-grandparents of that King David, and the direct ancestors of the greatest King of Israel, Jesus, Lord and God. Could they have had any idea how God would work through that chance meeting in a field?

And so it is for us. We do not know, and cannot see, how the little things we do on our frontlines might be tended by God and grow beyond any possible imagining. We begin by picking up litter, and the story ends we cannot see how.

Does God still act in this way? Does God still begin with one man or woman, as he began with Abraham and turned a childless, idolatrous nomad into the father of descendants as numerous as sand on the seashore? Might he still be a weaver of miracle and meaning over the centuries?

## A tale of two hats

It happened on the eighteenth day of October in the year of our Lord 2012 in the London borough of Islington.

But it began in the year of our Lord 1561. A London girl called Alice Wilkes is walking in a field in Islington, wearing a hat, as girls would have done at that time. She stops to watch some cows being milked. Over in another field some men are practising archery. One of them clearly needs the practice because a stray arrow ends up lodged in Alice Wilkes's hat. She is an inch or two from death.

In gratitude for sparing her life, Alice Wilkes makes a vow to the Lord. If one day she has wealth, she will do something for the poor. So she marries. And her husband dies. And she marries again. And her second husband dies. This is perhaps a dangerous woman to marry. Undeterred, Judge Thomas Owen becomes her third husband. And in the course of time he too dies.

By this point, Dame Alice Owen has acquired quite a lot of money and she decides to fulfil the vow she made when she was young Alice Wilkes. And so she endows a school for thirty scholars and creates alms houses for poor widows, women who were not so fortunate as to marry rich men. And when Alice dies, it is all put in trust with the Worshipful Company of Brewers.

Over 400 years later, the school she founded in Islington still educates children, though on a site in Potters Bar, and the land she gave has, for over 400 years, been used to generate income to bless the poor.

And so in the year of our Lord 2010, the Worshipful Company of Brewers decide to assign a building project to Thornsett Group, a smallish development company in London. Their assignment is to develop some mixed residential and commercial property, offering roughly half social housing and half private housing on the land that Alice Wilkes once walked across.

And so it is that on Thursday 18 October 2012 I find myself in Islington, going to meet the project developer who had been on one of LICC's courses, walking on the land where the cows once grazed and good Englishmen practised their archery.

And the person in charge of that overall development is called Bernadette. She just happens to be a Christian who comes from a family devoted to building good buildings so that people might flourish. When I meet her, she just happens to be wearing a hat, a hat altogether harder and more colourful than the decorative tissue that Alice Wilkes would have worn. Perhaps Bernadette was mindful of the fate of her predecessor and concerned about archers in Islington High Street, or then again, perhaps she was just following health and safety guidelines.

And as I look at Bernadette in her hat, working to bless the poor of Islington, I realize that God is still honouring the vow that Alice Wilkes made over 400 years before, still working through his people to bless others.

And I got to see it.

We don't always get to see how God may be working in us or in others, how a word here or an action there might produce fruit for years to come; we don't always get to see how we are participating in the purpose of God or how we might be the answers to other people's prayers . . . we don't get to see all the ways God might work through us . . .

The kingdom of heaven is like what? The kingdom of heaven is like a mustard seed which a man took and planted in his field and, though it is a small thing, a vow made 400 years ago, a little action today, a kindness, a decision, a word, a gift . . . 'Though it is the smallest of all seeds, yet when it grows, it is the largest of garden plants and becomes a tree, so that the birds come and perch in its branches' (Matthew 13:32). All our small things now, over time, who knows . . . who knows . . .

God is at work. And God has been at work in his people, in his church, in this land. And, no doubt, in you, in a myriad ways. We may not get to see the outcome in our lifetimes, but it is so.

And so, the Lord be with you, whatever hat you wear.

The Lord be with you on your frontline.

The Lord – the King of Glory, the Shield of David, the Friend of Sinners, the Redeemer of All, the Sovereign of Time, the Fount of all Wisdom, the Source of all Power, the Spring of all Love – be with you.

## Exploring further

Tim Chester and Steve Timmis, *Total Church: A Radical Reshaping around Gospel and Community* (Nottingham: IVP, 2007).

Neil Hudson, *Imagine Church: Releasing Whole-Life Disciples* (Nottingham: IVP, 2012).

Timothy J. Keller, *Center Church: Doing Balanced, Gospel-Centered Ministry in Your City* (Grand Rapids: Zondervan 2012).

Tim Morey, *Embodying Our Faith: Becoming a Living, Sharing, Practicing Church* (Downers Grove: IVP, 2009).

R. Paul Stevens, *Liberating the Laity: Equipping All the Saints for Ministry* (Vancouver: Regent College Publishing, 2002).

# GOOD NEWS FOR THE 98%. AND THE 2% TOO.

**About the London Institute for Contemporary Christianity**

The vast majority of Christians (around 98%) spend the vast majority of their waking time (around 95%) in non-church related activities. So just imagine what the impact might be on our neighbourhoods, on our schools and clubs and workplaces, on our whole nation if all of us were really able to help one another to make a difference for Christ right where we are, out on our daily frontlines.

That's LICC's focus: empowering Christians to make a difference in God's world, and envisioning and equipping church leaders to help them do it.

Founded by John Stott in 1982, and now led by Mark Greene, LICC's growing team seeks to combine biblical wisdom, cultural insight and practical ideas to offer individuals and ministers (the 2%) a wide range of resources. We speak, run courses and workshops, and offer consultancy to churches. And if you click on our website you'll find a trove of free material – clips, articles, downloads – as well as simple sign-ups for our themed prayer journeys and our punchy weekly emails – *Word for the Week* and *Connecting with Culture*.

So, if you're looking to make a greater difference where you are, or you'd like your church to become the kind of community that's committed to frontline mission, check out what's available online or get in touch.

W: www.licc.org.uk
E: mail@licc.org.uk
T: + 44 (0)20 7399 9555
Facebook ⓕ: Like us at facebook.com/LICCLtd
Twitter ⓣ: Follow us on Twitter@LICCLtd

St Peter's Church, Vere Street, London, W1G 0DQ

licc make a difference where you are

## also available

# Fruitfulness on the Frontline – the DVD

ISBN: 978-0-9928190-0-2
8 sessions

*'Extremely helpful in broadening my understanding of what it means to follow Jesus in the real world.'* Galen

We all need other people to help us grow, and this eight-session DVD is a brilliant way to explore the 6Ms further with Christian friends and/or work colleagues – to go deeper, share ideas, apply the principles and support one another. With lots of new, true stories about people making a difference on the frontline, the resource combines biblical teaching from Mark Greene, creative graphics and online access to a whole bagful of free extra material including:

- Leader's session guide with carefully crafted questions
- Additional filmed stories
- A specially developed 40-day prayer journey
- Preaching guides for church leaders

*'As a group, we were really able to relate what we were learning to our frontlines. It gave us (lots of) practical ideas of things that we could do.'* Karen, group leader

*'The group left feeling encouraged and inspired. We found it particularly helpful to be reminded that we are living in freedom in Christ and the 6M's are not a holy to-do list to feel guilty about, but are enablers and reminders.'* Neil, group leader

*'A fantastic resource – it provided clear structure and direction for our group – and a great tool for those leading the discussion who had never done it before. Everyone contributed and got involved.'* Emily, group leader

Available from your local Christian bookshop or **www.thinkivp.com**

# Imagine Church
*Releasing whole-life disciples*
Neil Hudson

ISBN: 978-1-84474-566-1
192 pages, paperback

How can an ordinary church grow disciples who live their whole lives as followers of Jesus? Disciples whose faith shapes their attitudes as neighbours, colleagues and family members?

Our time in church needs to equip us to be salt and light in our time out there. Drawn from the hard-won lessons of the Imagine project, this book offers help and hope from churches which have begun to do just that:

- Lessons from three years' work with pilot churches
- Practical ideas for your church
- Real-life stories of churches and individuals

It doesn't offer quick fixes. There aren't any. Instead, it offers new hope and little changes that change everything.

*'The idea of whole-life discipleship could hardly be more important. This stimulating book is both thoughtful and immensely practical. I highly recommend it to anyone with a leadership role.'* Stephen Gaukroger

What we hear in church on Sunday morning sometimes seems worlds away from the challenges we face on Monday morning. The **FAITH AT WORK** series helps us make vital connections between God and our work.

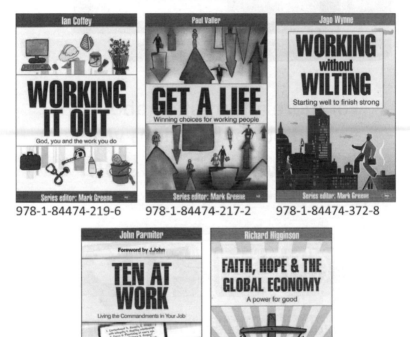

978-1-84474-219-6   978-1-84474-217-2   978-1-84474-372-8

978-1-84474-557-9   978-1-84474-580-7

Inter-Varsity Press

For more information about IVP
and our publications visit
**www.ivpbooks.com**

Get regular updates at **ivpbooks.com/signup**
Find us on **facebook.com/ivpbooks**
Follow us on **twitter.com/ivpbookcentre**

Inter-Varsity Press, a company limited by guarantee registered in England and Wales, number 05202650. Registered
office IVP Bookcentre, Norton Street, Nottingham NG7 3HR, United Kingdom. Registered charity number 1105757.